Preaching
in the
Great Tradition

Preaching in the Great Tradition

NEGLECTED CHAPTERS
IN THE HISTORY OF PREACHING

The Samuel A. Crozer Lectures for 1949

RAY C. PETRY

Professor of Church History, Duke University

Philadelphia
THE WESTMINSTER PRESS

*To All Who Love Crozer
and to Their Christian Fellows Everywhere
Preaching in the Great Tradition*

CONTENTS

PREFACE

THIS book treats of neglected aspects in the history of preaching. It is designed to serve as a companion volume to my source edition, *No Uncertain Sound: Sermons That Shaped the Pulpit Tradition,* The Westminster Press, 1948. The primary texts and critical apparatus of that work support and illustrate the fresh contributions of this study. The present work facilitates the effective use of that anthology.

The materials of this volume comprise, with slight modifications, the lectures delivered on the Samuel A. Crozer Foundation, at Crozer Theological Seminary. The dedication expresses in some measure my deep gratitude for the gracious hospitality extended me by Dr. Edwin E. Aubrey, then president of Crozer; Dean Charles Batten; the faculty, students, alumni, trustees, and all others of the Crozer community during March 15–17, 1949.

I express appreciation to the staff of The Westminster Press, for generous editorial assistance; to my colleagues in the Divinity School of Duke University, as well as to Professors Martin Rist, of the Iliff School of Theology; Alan Swallow, of the University of Denver; and S. Harrison Thomson, of the University of Colorado, for scholarly counsel and academic courtesies; to Mrs. Hollis W. Huston, for secretarial aid; and to my wife, Ruth Mertz Petry, for many services distinctively rendered.

Grateful acknowledgment is made to the following publishers for permission to quote from copyrighted materials. For the right to reproduce sections from *No Uncertain Sound*, I am indebted to The Westminster Press, Philadelphia. Translated passages involving Origen, and the " four senses " of Scripture, are drawn, respectively, from R. B. Tollinton, *Selections from the Commentaries and Homilies of Origen*, 1929, and Robert M. Grant, *The Bible in the Church: A Short History of Interpretation*, 1948; all copyrighted by, and used by permission of, The Macmillan Company, publishers. Selections from Berthold of Regensburg, translated in G. G. Coulton, *Life in the Middle Ages*, four volumes in one, Cambridge: At the University Press, 1930, are reproduced with the permission of the publishers. Extracts from Wulfstan are reprinted, by permission of the publishers, from Albert Stanbrough Cook and Chauncey Brewster Tinker, *Select Translations from Old English Prose*, Cambridge, Massachusetts: Harvard University Press, 1908. Passages from the canons of the Fourth Lateran Council, 1215, are translated by H. J. Schroeder, *Disciplinary Decrees of the General Councils*, and used by permission of B. Herder Book Co., St. Louis, Missouri. Selected portions from *The Sermons and Conferences of John Tauler, of the Order of Preachers*, . . . in the First Complete English Translation . . . by the Very Rev. Walter Elliott, of the Paulist Fathers, are reproduced by permission of the Rev. Richard S. Cartwright, C.S.P., for the publishers, The Apostolic Mission House, Brookland Station, Washington, D. C. Acknowledgment for the use of quotations from Father Paschal Robinson, *The Writings of St. Francis of Assisi*, is made to The Dolphin Press, Philadelphia. The quotation from Nicholas of Cusa, *The Vision of God*, translated by Emma Gurney Salter, with an Introduction by Evelyn Underhill, is used by permission of the publisher, E. P. Dutton & Co., Inc., New York.

Source passages drawn from *No Uncertain Sound* (NUS) are identified by sermon number and page and are inserted parenthetically after the quotations reproduced: viz., (31:261).

Certain basic sources here analyzed or quoted are not translated in NUS but are, in most instances, listed in its critical Bibliography. To facilitate location of, and repeated reference to, such sources, they are given below according to the pages of this work in which they appear and with parenthetic reference to page numbers of the annotated Bibliography in NUS: viz., (Bibliog., 313).

Pages 32–35. Preaching hazards are analyzed from sources reconstructed in *La chaire française*, by L. Bourgain (Bibliog., 320).

Pages 35, 53–58. Augustine's *On Christian Doctrine* is quoted after Marcus Dods's translation in Vol. IX of *The Works*, Edinburgh: T. and T. Clark, 1873.

Pages 46 f., 71 f., 101. Chrysostom's *On the Priesthood* is quoted from W. R. W. Stephens' translation in *The Nicene and Post-Nicene Fathers*, Vol. IX, 1st. Ser. (Bibliog., 313).

Pages 60 f. Paraphrases from Chapter I of Thomas Waleys' *De modo componendi sermones* are based on the edition of the *Artes praedicandi*, by Th.-M. Charland (Bibliog., 313).

Pages 74–78. Jacques de Vitry's sermons, especially the first to priests and prelates, are in the edition, *Selecta ex sermonibus vulgaribus*, by Cardinal Pitra (Bibliog., 316).

Page 75. Digests of Alain de Lille follow his *Summa* (Bibliog., 311).

Pages 78, 105 f. Humbert de Romans is analyzed from the Berthier and De La Bigne editions of his *De eruditione praedicatorum* (Bibliog., 315).

Page 84. Gregory's *Morals* are quoted in the J. H. Parker edition of Charles Marrott, Oxford, 1844.

Pages 87 f. Sermon "examples" are analyzed after *L'ex-*

emplum, by J. T. Welter (Bibliog., 325).

Pages 90–93. De Bourbon is interpreted from his *Anecdotes* (Bibliog., 314) and Bromyard from his *Summa* (Bibliog., 313).

Pages 106–114. Wyclif analyses follow the *Sermones, De veritate sacrae scripturae,* and *Opus evangelicum* in the Latin editions of the Wyclif Society and Thomas Arnold's edition of the *Select English Works* (Bibliog., 319).

RAY C. PETRY.

INTRODUCTION

THE Church historian, no less than his colleague in the field of homiletics, must accept some responsibility for the neglect into which the history of preaching has fallen. Fresh acquaintance with the virtually unclaimed legacy of pre-Reformation preaching serves at least one end. Such research for a still recoverable heritage provides the means of appropriating anew, in our own age, the continuing tradition of gospel proclamation.

The sermonic record of a versatile Christian ministry during fifteen hundred years of pre-Reformation history is appreciated almost exclusively today by a handful of linguistic experts and students of secular culture. The spiritual descendants of the preachers in the Great Tradition have proved not so much scornful as unaware of this cumulative gospel testimony. In a fashion that often shames our listless effort, these followers of the apostle Paul gave forth " no uncertain sound." Weak and strong, fainthearted and iron-willed, they heeded well the injunction in Isa. 58:1: " Cry, cease not, lift up thy voice like a trumpet, and show my people their wicked doings, and the house of Jacob their sins."

Surely there is no area of preparation and service in which the seminaries and the churches can support each other more gladly than in the rediscovery of the Christian evangel, the reinvestment of ministerial heritage within the fellowship of the Great Tradition.

Preaching
in the
Great Tradition

Chapter One

THE CHRISTIAN HERITAGE
AND MINISTERIAL RESPONSIBILITY

A S WE begin the task of rediscovering the Christian preaching of the Great Tradition in the pre-Reformation period, the first thing that should command our attention is the ministers' sense of responsibility to preach. The most devoted servants of the Lord, the ages through, have felt keenly their responsibility as preachers and teachers to proclaim the good news of Christ. Brilliant or plodding; humble or influential; learned or handicapped — they conceived of the gospel entrusted to them to be preached as the rock on which they must stand or the stone by which they would be ground to powder. It was, for them, the unique good news of God's Kingdom. Through them, this gospel was to be preached and lived as the sole way of salvation for men, women, and children, slaves and kings, Greeks and barbarians. Responsibility for such proclamation of Word and life devolved in some limited degree upon every Christian. But a special, awesome accountability for its announcement fell upon preachers of the Word and teachers of Christian doctrine.

The precise obligation of specific Christian leaders for such a declaration varied significantly according to the viewpoints of different preachers and periods, before the Reformation and afterward. But in a real sense Christian preachers, the centuries through, have put the gospel and its deliverance first, however varied their methods for doing so may have been. To call even a limited roll of testimony from among them is to regain a lost perspective and to find new courage for our own tasks. Jesus preached God's Kingdom and sent his disciples out to do likewise. Paul placed a sacrificial ministry to the world above baptism or any other pursuit, however laudable. Preaching Christ crucified and risen from the dead became his constant preoccupation. Then ordinary men of the ancient Church, transforming the world by extraordinary acts of the Spirit, preached like Peter, until men asked, " What shall we do to be saved? " Saint Augustine, like Chrysostom, found in the Scriptures the central way of life. These homilists exercised in the preaching-teaching ministry a vocation from God to declare Christ to every condition of mankind. Like many others, they trembled at their awful responsibility. But they feared even more the consequences of shirking their clear duty.

The humble scholar Bede the Venerable, who died in 735, spent his entire life in Scriptural researches and other religious duties within a circumscribed geographical area. But his ministry is woven into all our lives, whether we recognize it or not. Francis of Assisi in the thirteenth century discovered in Christ his only master and preached the gospel as the only true rule of life. John Wyclif, fiery English teacher and indefatigable preacher, made " Goddis Lawe " the one constitutional requisite for a new world in the fourteenth. He insisted that this law be stamped on every man's conscience and that it move in every human heart. He called for fellow scholars and students to help to translate it into the vernacular; for Christians of every station and degree — not a few bishops and priests only — to carry it on the tips of their tongues and to shout it from every housetop.

Who doesn't know at second hand (how much more thrilling to have learned firsthand!) how Luther preached an old world into the discard and a new order into the forefront of history? And what would colonial and frontier America, as well as evangelical Britain, have been without the stern trumpeting of Fuller, Edwards, Whitefield, Tennent, Cartwright, and hosts more?

Such men viewed the demands of the Christian gospel in all their exacting fullness. The medieval Church might regard the bishop as having a special responsibility and prerogative for preaching. Some medieval preachers, and many later ones, would give the bishop added responsibility but no greater privileges. Ancient, medieval, and Reformation churches recognized the versatile resources of the gospel and called for a wide range of ministries to support and advance it. A third-century scholar, Origen, labored in his classroom to clarify the evangelical message. Twelfth-century deacons helped to serve the Scriptural word at the altar, as the priests served it more widely in their parish pulpits. Monastic copyists, vowed to silence, transmitted the living word with their hands, even though their voices were not heard. Teachers of liturgical music as well as technicians of the sermonic arts advanced the same gospel. Leonardo da Vinci with his reincarnation of the Lord's Supper; Clément Marot in his adapting of the psalms to the singing heart; Charles Wesley and his hymns of praise; as well as Johannes Brahms, with his ineffable " Requiem," suggest alike the breadth, width, and depth of the Christian gospel. Each in his own way discharged an exacting responsibility through his own type of ministry.

These, and many others more conventionally commissioned to preach, shouldered the terrifying responsibility of proclaiming the full gospel. This meant searching the Scripture in all its senses. Involved also was the meticulously careful construction and practiced delivery of the sermon. The ministerial duty of joining Word and worship and sacraments and

preaching in the integrity of Christian experience was an inescapable responsibility. The ministries of mouth and heart
applied to the everyday routine of pastoral care also had to
be welded. And such a preaching-parish ministry meant un-
interrupted service to all groups: rich and poor, soldiers and
farmers, medical students and seminarians, sophisticated nobility and craven serfs, frightened serving girls and arrogant
knights.

The noblest apologists of a fearsome, yet joyous, priesthood
were such men as Saint Augustine, author of that too-little-
known book *On Christian Doctrine;* Chrysostom, eloquent pro-
tagonist of a complete gospel adequate to actual social situations and real human beings; Gregory Nazianzen, ancient
satirist of ventriloquist rumblings and proponent of a gospel
from the Lord's own mouth; and Humbert de Romans, great
Dominican preacher and writer of sermon manuals, who demonstrated equally well the Word needed for high churchmen,
skeptical law students, and busy men of the world.

Familiar to these and countless others were the tricky de-
tours and inspiring glory roads of the preaching ministry.
Well known to them also were the usual deterrents to faithful
preaching. Inadequate preparation and the lack of will to
correct it were always at hand. Pride in all its subtle forms
stood waiting. Fear of ridicule and persecution did its deadly
work. Episcopal lethargy and hostility were all too real. The
vanity of men who wished to compete with more popular
speakers entered into the story. Oratorical racketeering, which
commercialized unauthorized platitudes for private gain, was
a verifiable fact.

But, however prominent the saboteurs of the gospel might
have been, the supporters of the true evangelism were by no
means lacking. Eloquent, effective preaching and the constantly reiterated appeal for better homiletics came from the

most diverse quarters. The first Pope Gregory was not a scholar in any real sense, but he left some of the most power-ful pleas for prophetic watchmanship yet heard. The imperial court and the Christian schools of Charles the Great gave a surprising impetus to gospel preaching and teaching. A good, hard-hitting pastor and eleventh-century crusader, Raoul Ar-dent, showed how charity and scholarly severity can serve the whole community in a fruitful gospel ministry.

Numerous ecumenical council chambers, from the Lateran to Lambeth, from Madras to Amsterdam, have pleaded for a rebirth of gospel propagation. Reformation schools, from the days of Melanchthon to the renascent centers of European Christian revival today, have called for renewed preaching and have taught it by precept and example. The exponents of systematic homiletics and sound theological exhortation have included Calvin, the Wesleys, unnamed frontier giants, and scholarly archbishops of Canterbury in our own day. In many a modern university, distinguished otherwise by its scientific detachment alone, some peer of the pulpit has galvanized academic pygmies into potential candidates for the Lord's horsemen.

THE INESCAPABLE VOCATION FROM GOD

We turn now to a more intensive examination of our preach-ing heritage: to the sense of responsibility as illustrated by the preachers themselves. Sometimes implicit, often explicit, was their periodic rediscovery of an awful, inescapable voca-tion from God! Well might the brilliant Origen ruminate, in the third century, upon these sobering words of Num. 25:4:

" *Take all the chiefs of the people and expose them unto the Lord over against the sun, and the anger of the Lord shall be turned away from Israel.*" " See," he says, " what is the lot of the leaders of the people; they are not only put on trial for their own offences, they are also compelled to give account for the sins of the people. Perhaps it is their fault that the people offends. Perhaps they did not teach, they did not warn, they did not take the trouble to convict those who had been the first to do wrong, so as to prevent the spread of the malady to others. The performance of these duties is laid upon leaders and teachers " (3:48–49). And how closely related, how frequently identified, were teaching and preaching, we shall have ample occasion to observe in Chapter Two.

Saint Augustine, whose treatise *On Christian Doctrine* might well be required reading for every student in hermeneutics and homiletics — not to mention Church history, Biblical literature, and theology — devotes virtually his whole fourth book to the means whereby the preacher and teacher may properly discharge their great calling. This too will receive extended treatment, subsequently.

In the late sixth century the first Pope Gregory, preaching on Ezek. 3:8, sighs reflectively over that noble preacher who said, " I am clear from the blood of all men, for I have not spared to declare unto you all the counsel of God " (Acts 20:26, 27). Gregory himself continues: " If he had not proclaimed it, surely he would not have been stainless. But he was free from the blood of those to whom he was zealous to announce all the counsel of God. By this word we are summoned to trial; we are fettered; we are shown to be guilty, we who are called priests, who, to our own ills, add the deaths of others; for we kill all those whom everyday we, lukewarm and silent, see going to their death." Gregory declares yet further, " And he who does not study to be zealous in preaching is made a partner in damnation " (15:96–97, 101).

Four and one half centuries later and thousands of preachers farther on — many of them quoting Gregory's words —

comes the author of the *Gomorrah*. Peter Damian, who died one year before his friend became Gregory VII in 1073, dedicated his sulphurous book to the memories, forever damned, of clergy who did *not* preach to the people their sins. In one of his sermons, suffused with irenic allegory, he celebrates the good deeds of Christ's disciples as they plodded to the village to find an ass and its colt. Damian patiently explains what we must impatiently reject, namely, that by the ass and colt tied in the village " are signified the people of the Jews, and that of the Gentiles, both of them in bondage to the chain of their sins. . . . The two disciples sent into the village are the preachers of the two Testaments, endued with twofold charity, the love of God and the love of our neighbour; or else Peter and Paul, of whom one was the Apostle of the Jews, the other of the Gentiles. . . . These loosed both people from the error of infidelity, and, by the word of their preaching, brought them to the faith of Jesus Christ " (22:126).

Innocent III, that thirteenth-century pontiff of cultured argument and virile commands, preaches a strange discourse on Luke 5:3-6: " Launch out into the deep and let down your nets for a draught." He gives a brief course in Biblical criticism, levies upon the legendary foundation of Rome, and comes up with this curious summation: Peter and Paul both " let down their nets of preaching to catch men in the city " of Romulus and Remus (34:178). Through preaching in that city founded by two brothers according to the flesh, two brothers of the faith let down their nets. By that preaching " Rome was converted from error to truth, from sins to virtues " (34:180). Without going surety for such tortured interpretation we may remark in this sermon, as in so many others, a seriousness concerning the preaching function that few of us can match.

Ironical in the extreme is the fact that this same Innocent

did more for preaching through his ambiguous approval of Francis of Assisi's voluntary witnessing than in the specific canons of his cherished Council of the Fourth Lateran. For Francis did what Innocent held in realistic dubiety: he exalted " the balm-bearing words of . . . [the] Lord " (35:182) as a feasible answer to daily problems and helped properly authorized brethren to " make the Lord's word short on the earth." With typical naïveté, the *Poverello* counseled brief sermons to men and women whose time for repentance had, he felt, all but run out.

Bonaventura, the great Franciscan scholastic and mystic, did not scruple to designate as the noblest of all hierarchical functions the preaching of God's Kingdom; to this same office Christ had declared himself sent. Humbert de Romans, a thirteenth-century Dominican contemporary in piety, scholarship, and administration, enlarged in more eloquent fashion than Bonaventura upon the indispensability and inexorable demands of the preaching ministry. To his sober words of warning we shall later return.

John Wyclif, who died in 1384, was the admiring commentator of Francis' rule and his apostolic preaching; even as he was the inveterate enemy of Francis' later followers. This same Wyclif, as will appear in due time, placed such bald emphasis upon the preaching responsibility as virtually to stand alone in the whole of the Middle Ages.

THE RESPONSIBILITY OF BISHOPS FOR PREACHING

From early times the bishops enjoyed special prerogatives and responsibilities in preaching, but priests and others to whom the episcopacy delegated homiletic functions came to play an enlarging role in this duty. Wyclif and a few others of the medieval period strenuously denied that the bishop alone preached by right of office. Nonetheless, the established practice from quite early times seems to have given preaching ascendancy to the *episcopos*, who would duly license such presbyters as he saw fit, and, in rare instances, permit some limited hortatory rights to deacons. The other side of the medieval case for the episcopal pre-eminence was the bishop's responsibility to preach to the limit of his powers and to raise up assistants for whose preaching effectiveness he was fully answerable.

All cardinal sources of the medieval period show rigid insistence, from a theological and canonical viewpoint, on the episcopal obligation to preach. Church law, summarized in Gratian's *Decretum*, bluntly indicates the bishop's responsibility to study the Scriptures and to teach them. Stephen of Tournai also tersely represents the episcopal prerogative and consequent obligation. Bishops were often chosen, as Mandonnet notes, on the basis of preaching merit — over and above any and all administrative talents. As already observed, the bishop was not asked to assume his frightening task alone. His original prerogative was shared, at his own request, with other prelates and ordinaries, that is, abbots, superiors, and others. According to Peter Cantor, country pastors were definitely within the ranks of those asked, upon occasion, to assist the bishop in this work. Peter Damian specifically approves the inclusion of priests in the preaching order — Christ sent out not only the Twelve but also the Seventy. Anselm pictures Peter walking on the sea to receive Jesus' commendation as one of the order of preachers who hasten to lead the faithful to the Kingdom of Heaven.

The twelfth century shows an upsurge, and the thirteenth marks a high peak, in the sharing of this episcopal function with others commissioned according to proper authorization. To be sure, Innocent III sharply reminds the laity that they cannot pick their own preachers. These must be chosen by the authorized clergy from the ranks of a select few. Councils see to it that bishops do call others to aid them in the well-nigh impossible task of redressing the lagging fortunes of good preaching. Intensive researches show how temporary revivals such as those of the Carolingian period were all too regularly followed by marked decadence. Regular preaching on Sunday — a practice observed quite early at certain places — was not imposed as an obligation generally until the Council of Trent in the sixteenth century. By the end of the twelfth century, however, provincial assemblies are reminding priests to have their people recite the paternoster, credo, and ave, and to explain such prayers to the congregation. How lacking at best was their emphasis on the gospel is clearly apparent in the rueful admonitions of Grosseteste and the subsequent laments of Peckham.

Francis of Assisi is typical of those devout sons of Mother Church who thought of preaching as being carried on always within the framework of the episcopal pattern. He states categorically, " Let none of the brothers preach contrary to the form and institution of the holy Roman Church." The brethren were not to preach in any diocese against the will of its bishop. Nevertheless, as we well know, generous papal approval made later Franciscan and Dominican preaching an effective, expanded function.

Wyclif was quick enough to stress the unique accountability of the bishop for the cure of souls; but he hastened to insist that bishops had no greater right than any priest, or, indeed, any Christian, to proclaim " Goddis Lawe."

Although remaining a loyal son of the Church, Michel Menot, a French Minorite contemporary with Luther's rise, was almost as pungent as Wyclif, or Doctor Martin, in his criticism of delinquent prelates. He was well-nigh as dedicated as Francis, or Paul, in declaring, " Woe is unto me if I preach not the gospel." The Assisan had demanded Franciscan preaching in language purified as by fire that should edify the people and announce to them "vices and virtues, punishment and glory." Reminiscent of this is Michel's answer to Isaiah's query, "What shall I cry?" The reply is: "To the just, glory. To penitent sinners, pardon. And to those persisting in evil, eternal damnation" (60:308).

The Prophetic Call to Sinners

With the theme of prophetic challenge, wherein sinners are called to repentance, ere judgment fall and the Kingdom come, there is need to poll the shapers of the Great Tradition further.

Chrysostom, sympathetically yet prophetically identified with a sinful people as few preachers have been, cries out: "Oh! that it were possible that I could perform good works as your substitute, and that you could receive the rewards of those works! . . . The thing is impossible; for to every man will . . . [God] render according to his own works, . . . on That Day, when ye are called to judgment, I shall not be able to assist you" (6:67).

Wulfstan, archbishop of York in the early eleventh century, placed the Lord's ax at the root of decaying social mores with a boldness hardly exceeded in English history: "Dearly beloved, understand the truth: this world is in haste, and drawing nigh the end. Hence is the later in the world ever the worse, so that things must needs wax very evil before the coming of Antichrist. Likewise, consider earnestly that for these many years the devil has led this people too widely astray; that men have held little faith towards one another, for all their fair speaking; that injustice has too much prevailed in the land; and that they have been few who thought upon a remedy as diligently as they ought. Daily has evil been heaped

upon evil, and men have worked iniquity and manifold un-
righteousness far too generally throughout this whole nation"
(21:122). And Wulfstan goes on to demonstrate that a man
with such an expectancy of the end of the world as his may
well become, not less concerned with, but more aroused to,
the need of temporal action properly anticipating the coming
of the eternal Kingdom.

Jean Gerson was an extraordinary scholar, conciliarist, and
versatile French preacher of repentance. He marveled publicly that Saint Peter, chosen the earthly head of Christ's own
Church, should have fallen a prey to such humiliation as his
denial of the Lord entailed. "Take a lesson from this," he says
to his enthralled audience, " as to how a great public sinner, in
the past, was able to be a preacher of truth and good (Christian) life. But this had to come afterwards and with penitence,
bitter and public; otherwise it could not have been possible.
You see this in Saint Peter who sinned before, and afterwards
preached and governed the Church; but this also was after
penitence." Thus it was, the preacher explains, that a man made
to wince every time he heard a rooster crow, yet came again to
look his Master in the face. Concluding his sermon, as always,
with a prayer, Gerson pleads: "And You, sweet Jesus, true
Savior of all the world, look upon Your little serfs and subjects, whatever their age and sex may be; look at them now
with that look with which You looked on Saint Peter and let it
be that always they may have, through penitence, their sins in
remembrance " (53:268).

And, even as European voyagers were discovering new
worlds without, Savonarola called for the renovation of the
old Adam from within. " O sinners, stubborn, lukewarm, all
who defer repentance to the last, . . . do penance; do it now;
do not delay any longer, for the Lord now awaits you and thus
He calls you. Listen to my words, not as if they came from me,

but from God. . . .

" Your sins, then, O Italy, O Rome, O Florence, your im-
pieties, your fornications, your cruelties, your sins, I say, be-
get these tribulations. Here is the cause! And if you have
found the cause of all this evil, look for its remedy. Eradicate
the sin that is the source of it, and you will be healed. . . .

" O rich, O poor, do penance; and you rich, give alms to the
poor. . . .

" O consecrated priests, hear my words, O priests, O prelates of the Church of Christ, renounce your benefices that you
cannot serve; renounce your pomp and your convivial gatherings and the banquets which you give so splendidly; renounce,
I say, your concubines and your boys, for it is time I say to do
penance. . . .

" O monks, renounce the extravagance of your attire and
your silver vessels and the over-running fatness of your ab-
beys and benefices. . . .

" O nuns, renounce, renounce you, too, your extravagances;
. . . renounce your florid chants. . . .

" O merchants, renounce your usuries. . . .

" And now, O priests, I must come back to you; I mean the
bad ones, for I am always reverent to the good ones. Renounce, I say, that unspeakable vice . . . that has so greatly
provoked the wrath of God upon you. If you do not, woe, woe,
to you! "

Useless it was for such a man to say, " You should realize
by this time that I speak to you as a father to his children,
for your good; and you should see that God, in this affliction
of yours, has given me to you as a father, to show you the way
to correct your errors, that you may merit forgiveness in the
judgment of God " (59:296–299). Columbus, the " Admiral of
the Ocean Sea," had brought back too little gold, and he was
disciplined. Savonarola had opened up the old festering sore

of man's sin. For that — in part, at least — and not only for his political indiscretions, he died.

THE PROCLAMATION OF FORGIVING LOVE

Yet it was not for this thundering of prophetic doom alone that the Lord's messengers arose. Theirs was the joyous responsibility also for proclaiming God's seeking, forgiving love; a saving love to be appropriated freely by man in faith.

Augustine, preaching on the theme of Jer. 31:33, " I will give my law in their viscera, and I will write it upon their heart," says: " He who has called you to His kingdom and glory will grant to you who are born again by His grace that these words be written in your hearts by the Holy Spirit, in order that you may love because you believe, and that faith may work through love " (13:89–90). For, as the bishop had just said: " Through this faith you hope for grace in which all sins will be forgiven you. By this you will be saved, and not of yourselves, for this is the gift of God (Rom. 6:23)."

Bernard of Clairvaux, likewise, with a remarkable adaptation of Canticles 3:1, insists that the soul, seeking God, is anticipated by him. " *I have sought*, says the Bride, *Him whom my soul loveth*. It is to this that the goodness of Him who has anticipated you in seeking you and loving you first, it is to this that His goodness is calling and arousing you. You would not seek Him at all, O soul, nor love Him at all, if you had not been first sought and first loved " (30:165).

On this theme Guarric, Peter of Blois, and many others sing a jubilant refrain. And why could these preachers sound such an exultant, undistorted note of joy? Because, for them, as for us, though surely in ways and at times not always acceptable to our day, they put Christ first. Hear Origen as he rejoices:

" The greatness of our Saviour did not appear at the time when He was born, but now, after being apparently sup-

pressed by His opponents, it has shone out. . . . The power of
our Lord and Saviour is even with those who are cut off in
Britain from our world, with the inhabitants of Mauretania,
and with all under the sun who have believed in His name "
(1:46).

Or inquire of Peter Damian, the fearless castigator of man's
sins, mellow now, in reflection upon his Lord: " We must go
after Him, because He is the Truth, that we may not be de-
ceived; *through* Him, because He is the Way, that we may not
err; *to* Him, because He is the Life, that we may not die "
(23:127). That this is mere rhetoric, many of us would deny,
even as we affirm the centrality of his Christ.

Nicholas of Cusa — theologian, mathematician, philosopher,
linguist, and consecrated preacher of the fifteenth century —
bears this testimony to the *Christoformity* of the Christian's
life:

" But no one can enter into the way of grace, which leads
to the Father, through himself; he must enter through a gate.
Christ who proclaimed himself to be the gate is also the Way:
the faithful Christian, by the work of faith through love, enters
through the gate and finds himself in the Way. The gate is
faith. The Way is love. Thus faith in Christ becomes both gate
and Way " (58:294).

PREACHERS AS WATCHFUL SHEPHERDS

This message, then, the preacher must proclaim as the ever-
watchful shepherd of the whole flock. In this wise, Gregory
admonished the true curate of souls, the pastor of the sheep,
to meet the needs of those entrusted to him. For this cause
every preacher and teacher " ought to consider what he should
say, and to whom, and when, and how, and how much "
(15:98). The resultant homily is full of such good advice for
the minister to the whole parish that to read it once is to be

conscious always, in some degree, of one's pastoral frailty —
of one's standing forever " in the need of prayer."

When, around the year 1000, Ælfric the devout abbot
preached on the text of John 10:11, " I am the good pastor,"
he laid the memory of " Our Redeemer . . . the Good Shepherd " on every heart. Probably every outstanding preacher of
the Middle Ages had at least one sermon on that theme. Wyclif had at least two series — one in English and one in Latin
— developed with all the scorn for literary embellishment so
characteristic of him. Where Ælfric in prophetic modesty re-
fers briefly, if firmly, to bishops and teachers who are hirelings, Wyclif arms himself in head and chest, wrists and
thighs, for assault on all but the occasional " good " bishop
and priest of his day.

Inserted, chronologically, between Ælfric in the eleventh
century and Wyclif in the fourteenth is Bernard of Clairvaux,
with his canticle sermon on " How Careful, Watchful, and
Discreet Good Pastors Ought to Be in Feeding the Souls Given
Into Their Charge " (29:158). " Wherefore be ye watchful,"
he says, " whosoever of you have been chosen and called to
the work of this ministry; take watchful heed, I say, to yourselves, and to the precious deposit which has been entrusted
to you. It is a *city;* watch, then, to maintain it in safety and
concord. It is a *Bride;* study to present her to the Lord decked
with the precious jewels of abundant virtues. It is a *flock;*
study diligently to give it needful pasture " (29:160).

OBSTACLES TO TRUE PREACHING

To follow such advice was not easy. Obstacles on every hand
were placed in the way of the Lord's witnesses. Documents
emanating from the twelfth century recount the perils of witnessing for the gospel.

Dangers there are in plenty for the divine spokesman. Not

all hearers receive the message as a way to life; some there are for whom it is death. These last crush under foot the pearls of the gospel and devour the preachers of the Word. Yet others, profiting by the good news, praise those who publish it abroad and thus subject them to the dangers of pride. To this menace of hostility from one side, the preacher must oppose patience; against the vanity-engendering appreciation from the other, he must raise an impenetrable humility.

True, there are always those who rejoice in the preacher's assault upon others' sins. Those of elevated rank chortle at the poor man's discomfiture; the humble enjoy the embarrassment of the exalted. But let a preacher try to lay bare the faults of superiors and inferiors alike and he is in gathering trouble. He will be universally accused of madness and hounded into silence.

In these twelfth-century sources, as in others, the preachers chant a dolorous accusation: they are a constant prey to preacher-hating, gospel-calumniating detractors. Bishops, guilty of manifold disorders, do not take kindly to preachers who indict their irregularities. Rather would they transfer their culpability to exposers of their faults.

Not all, apparently, were so fortunate as the heroic Vital de Mortain, who, heckled and menaced by simoniacs, relied on the Lord's protection and faced down his accusers into full confession.

Lambert of Liege, inveighing against simony and concubinage, received a Christian hearing from the laity but fell victim to the clergy. They brought pressure on the bishop to silence "this mettlesome Apostle." Preaching one day in the Church of St. Martin, Lambert saw his accusers approaching. Before they had time to wreak their vengeance upon him, he hastened to predict that swine would soon root beneath the altar, until then consecrated to holy things. The bishop finally rescued him from continuing bodily injury and sent him into protective incarceration at a convenient château.

Some preachers fell heir to a fate still worse. Their ears itching for praise, they attuned their messages to popular favor and enjoyed rapidly accruing wealth. Other clerics, not content with parading their newly prostituted gifts, laid plans to corner the homiletic market, safe from monastic competitors. The crowning effrontery was the usurpation of the preaching office, not by conscientious exhorters like Peter Waldo, but by lay orators who organized a system of lucrative public exploitation and wholesale commercialization of the gospel.

Still, none of these difficulties was cause sufficient to dissuade the true evangelist from his divinely imposed vocation. Neither in the twelfth nor in the sixteenth century were all the Lord's dogs rendered mute, whether by happy dreams or by reason of mouths filled with bones. Like their barking, biting progenitors, there were those hardy gospel canines who bayed in full pursuit of the Church's enemies and brought to abject confusion many of its foes. Happily, the preachers' plaints against persecution and homiletic renegades are balanced by primary evidence of some witnesses in every age who evangelized the nations and proved worthy of the Lord's approval; yes, even to the martyr's crown.

Here is a close paraphrase of one such, namely, Geoffroy Babion, as he calls his fellow preachers to their task: The world is a Babylon. You must recall it to the right way. Yes, you must be in the van of this battle, this warfare. Preach! Preach! Prepare for preaching by the practice of virtues. Recall the sinner from the evil road by the energy of your words; it is your duty. Combat this Babylon by preaching. Waste not your public opportunity in vain conversation, but direct the Lord's army against Babylon. Remember your city, my brethren; defend Jerusalem. The enemy is innumerable and the good citizens — to what a paucity they are reduced! So, Geoffroy.

SHARERS IN THE PREACHERS' RESPONSIBILITIES

Some there were, like the Carthusians, who, committed to verbal silence, copied sermons and sermon books with indefatigable zeal. " Because we are not able to announce the Word of God with living voice," said one, " we do it with the hand."

Surely, those who remained constant in season and out of season, proclaiming the Lord's oracles, had a further duty which was, at the same time, a cherished opportunity. They could and did call the hearers of the Word, together with themselves, the preachers of it, to a common surrender before the Lord's will.

To his audience Chrysostom had turned with these words: " And now, it is time that you should be teachers and guides of others; that friends should undertake to instruct and lead on their neighbours; servants their fellow-servants; and youths those of their own age " (7:68). " Thinking therefore of these things, let us arouse ourselves; for if ye bring not your own endeavours to the task, every thing on our part is to no purpose " (6:66). To himself he speaks first; to his hearers he afterward calls, " Let us show forth then a new kind of life " (8:70).

What was it that Augustine was to say in *On Christian Doctrine?* " A great orator has truly said that an ' eloquent man must speak so as to teach, to delight, and to persuade.' . . . When, however, the truth taught is one that must be carried into practise, and that is taught for the very purpose of being practised, it is useless to be persuaded of the truth of what is said, it is useless to be pleased with the manner in which it is said, if it be not so learnt as to be practised."

With this free adaptation of Ciceronian rhetoric to Christian ends, Augustine wrestled manfully. His hearers would not listen urbanely, applaud genteelly, criticize condescendingly, and reserve their own commitments indefinitely, if the great African had his way. In a sermon designed for both preachers and hearers of the Word he frankly assesses the danger in which a preacher stands — not only the pompous declaimer but also the humble, God-fearing messenger. How easy, by comparison, it is for the listener to sit in detached judgment, saying, " I should like to know whether that man who is preaching to me does all that he himself hears or that he says to others " (12:86–87). To them the Pauline words of Augustine are like a dentist's drill on a tender nerve: " ' But to me it is a very small thing to be judged by you or by man's day ' " (I Cor. 4:3). True, he seems to be saying, you have the right to be critical up to a point: " If you think well of me, you praise me; if you think ill, you accuse me; but you do not excuse yourself " (12:87). What Augustine actually means is: You don't think you can escape your share of responsibility, do you, because I have malappropriated mine?

How great a relief it would be for the preacher to hold his tongue and thus avoid the natural pitfalls of his calling! " Yet," he reminds his hearers, " it is zeal for you which does not permit us to keep this precept. And you, therefore, should pray to support him whom you know to be endangered for your sakes " (12:86).

Fiery, lovable Raoul Ardent put it more plainly still:

" But, my brethren, when I look at our lives and the lives of those under our direction, I find few (and this is lamentable) either true preachers or true sheep. . . .

" If the pastors act like this, what do the sheep do? Certainly it is not strange if the members are afflicted in the affliction of the head. The duty of the sheep is to hear and obey. But today the sinful sheep are unwilling to hear their pastors. They merely say: ' The priest preaches to extract the cash.' Even if they listen, they are certainly not mindful of what they have heard. They do not wish to obey their pastor but to judge him " (24:130–131).

Whereupon the severe, loving, and generally beloved pastor proposes a solution:

" And now, my brethren, because we both have sinned [that is, both priest and people], let us both lament, let us both hasten to do penance. Let us, like good shepherds, endeavor to acquaint you with the Gospel teaching both by word and by example. And you also, like good sheep, endeavor constantly, by listening and obeying, to remember what you have heard " (24:131).

Perhaps only Bernardine of Siena, the fifteenth-century canonist and popular preacher, could come closer to grips with the problem than this.

He says in paraphrased substance: Do you people hearing me actually listen to me? Hardly! Do you know that without preaching the horrors of hell and the glories of heaven would be meaningless to you? I doubt it! " O woman! in the morning when thou comest to the fount of life and of the teaching of God, to the sermon, leave not your husband abed, or your son, or your brother, but see to it that you wake him out of his sleep, and see to it that he also cometh to hear that which if he be dead will restore him to life. O fellow-citizens! do you wish Siena to prosper? You tell me, yes. See to it then that you hear the word of God; have the ordinance proclaimed that not until after the sermon shall have been preached each morning shall any man open his shop. . . . O! I hear that fellow yonder who saith, I could earn a soldo in the morning." Bernardine here turns to answer this startled listener whose thoughts had been thoroughly outlined for him before he had been conscious of thinking them. But just then the preacher spies a nodding female. " Hast thou understood me, O woman, thou who sleepest over there? I fear not. I come here to bring you the word of God, and you settle yourselves to sleep, and I must break off my preaching to waken you out of your sleep." Meanwhile, that man yonder grumbles: " He hath little to do! " And worn out with speaking God's words and interpreting others' meanderings, the prophet of Siena does what everyone must sooner or later do — he invokes Augustine: " The woman or the man who goeth to a sermon and letteth the word of God pass by doth sin in as grievous a manner as that one who doth ask to receive communion and then through his carelessness doth let the host fall to the ground. But there is this difference, however, that carelessness is a venial sin, but this is a mortal sin, to have not the will to listen when you are able to hear " (54:271–272). So much for one sermon that " Treats of the Preacher and the Listener, and of the Part That Belongeth to Each."

A LIVING SYNTHESIS OF MINISTERIAL RESPONSIBILITY

If a living synthesis of such ministerial sensitivity to the divine vocation be sought, scarcely a better one can be found than that of II Timothy. Here apostleship under Christ is grounded in the divine will and God's enabling purpose. The preacher's timidity is exorcised by the God-given spirit of " power and love and self-control." This holy calling is accepted, not by virtue of man's ability, but with full confidence in God's victoriously redemptive purpose. Fear and despair are expelled in the joy of dispensing a gospel of grace, death-transcending life, and spirit-propelled truth. To this preaching apostolate the true Christian is appointed; yea, summoned. Without shame or self-consciousness he speaks, not his own puny opinions, but the certainties entrusted by the Lord for saving deliverance to the hopeless.

Herein the minister finds the pattern of sound words, the breath of the indwelling Spirit, the grace of the undefeatable Christ. Logically enough, the pastoral plea of II Timothy is for faith in the Lord's sustaining grace; single-minded, disciplined service to the great Captain of all souls; liberty-inspired teaching and preaching like Jesus' own. This is the stern, relentless, loving, uncluttered pronouncement of the Lord's preachers. Purified of self-seeking, rigidly guarded from distorted fawning and posing before any person, unimpressed by glib chattering, apt in the personalized translation of difficult truths — the preacher of the gospel serves his day and generation, in unhurried calm. He it is, who, in transforming faith and light, lent from above, searches the Scriptures for precious pearls as he accepts his share of teaching and witnessing to the Lord before men. Such are they, who, in the presence of God and the world-judging Christ whose Kingdom is sure, are exhorted to " preach the word, be urgent in season and out of season, convince, rebuke, and exhort, be unfailing in patience and in teaching." Such are those whose keen sense of responsibility for the living gospel it is ours to recover — whose voices have uttered with the boldness of the trumpet " no uncertain sound."

Chapter Two

PREACHING AND TEACHING
IN THE CHRISTIAN MINISTRY

T HE functions of preaching and teaching reinforce one
another in the Christian ministry. In Jesus they are intimately joined, never self-consciously separated. The
apostles at Pentecost, and after, preach and teach the gospel
of Christ. They instruct and empower their brethren. They
persuade and convert those outside. Prophesying and teaching
are complementary almost to the point of popular identification. The Gospels — especially Matthew — are predicated
upon, and issue in, teaching as well as preaching. Preachers
in every productive Christian period know that they are help-
less without doctrine. Teachers know that their Christian instruction must result in preaching if it is to reach its mark.

Christian preaching and teaching develop most fruitfully
when they are learned and practiced in productive fellowship.
Then teaching is rescued from wooden aloofness and supercil-
iousness, and preaching is protected from vacuity and undisciplined ranting.

Teaching, it is true, puts rightful emphasis upon reason-
able detachment, objective assessment, unimpassioned inquiry.
Fields are delimited, methods are scrutinized, counterviews are
elicited. Disagreement, debate, and cautious balancing of fac-
tors are encouraged.

Preaching gives itself with equal propriety to clarifying issues, assessing moral and spiritual responsibilities, and pressing for social and individual decisions. Within its domain, men are brought to worship and nerved for action; concepts and attitudes are renovated; loyalties are evoked; ultimatums are delivered; commitments are demanded. The preacher entices, dares, persuades, and judges in the name of the Lord.

Yet, joined in the indisseverable alliance of Christian service, both preachers and teachers seek the truth at its source — prayerfully, critically, constructively. They inquire within themselves and outside themselves. It is imperative that, together, they listen before they speak, to hear what they shall say; and listen after they speak, to learn whether or not they have said it. Probing, researching, reflecting, and re-examining should find ready welcome from both. Preachers and teachers alike need to question in order to stand more firmly; they do well to stand for the right to question. Each in his distinctive way may be expected to elicit, discipline, and inspire. Neither preacher nor teacher can rightfully pre-empt the focusing of visions, nor claim sole credit for instilling aspirations and dedications. Together, they ought to proclaim fearlessly, yet grow steadily in humility and reverence. United, they may hope to call for loyalties that transcend individuals and groups alike, as well as all plans and wishes purely human. Thus coordinated in their distinctive differences and common allegiances they may surmount paralyzing tentativeness and prophetic affectation with commitment to the terms of Christ's gospel.

Scriptural instruction makes for preaching power. Augustine's study *On Christian Doctrine* reveals the storehouse of the gospel always waiting the preacher's periodic return. Savonarola's researching in the Bible is what led to his intrepid attack, almost singlehanded, on social perversion and ecclesiastical corruption in Italy. Rauschenbusch's resort to the

Biblical depositories of the faith eventuated in unexpected re-definitions of Christian problems and powers.

Cultivation of the mind does have its part in the cure of the soul. Bishop Grosseteste in the thirteenth century cautioned his intellectual wards, the Franciscans, against the chaotic emotionalism and undisciplined preaching that had made many monastic predecessors vapid and pitiful. Of course, to a non-resident pastor who had become a perennial graduate student but never a graduate curate the bishop finally wrote a stiff letter; but the occasion demanded the action taken.

Francke in his orphan house and Bible-study center at Halle revealed to his students, at one and the same time, the fountains of piety and the way of ministering to human necessities. Few, indeed, have joined intellectual discipline to menial, routine services for the good of humble people as has the learned musician, theologian, philosopher, and missionary Schweitzer.

Preaching in the churches and teaching in the seminaries are surely committed to a common cause. The teacher's inquiry becomes the preacher's resource. The teacher's sources are the preacher's wellsprings. Rightly did Luther and Wesley, Spurgeon and Fosdick, exemplify those lessons. The doctrinal systematizer has often been the preacher's rescuer. Good preaching needs sound theology as a worship service needs prayer.

But the dependence is by no means one-sided. The inspiration for the teacher in the school is the pastor and preacher in the field — the missionary and Christian world citizen in the parish of the whole earth. The goal of the teacher is the kind of articulate preaching and living of the Christ that must be tested among the people. This it is that has lifted the vision of the seminaries unto the eternal hills and given preachers in training their clue to genuine greatness. Divinity schools and churches are the inseparable proving grounds of the Lord. The disciplines of the classroom are validated in the highways and hedges. The fellowship of the chapel is spiritually enlarged by those, near and far, who have gone, and still go, from undivided worship of the divine to the unreserved ministry of the human.

THE INTIMATE ASSOCIATION OF PREACHERS AND TEACHERS

How intimately this conjunction of teaching and preaching is sustained in the Great Tradition may be illustrated by several examples. Origen, by his very spirit and intellectual formation, is a teacher. His great tasks are those of researching, testing, rejecting, and interpreting. His homilies deal in large part with the problems raised by the educating Deity and his student-creatures. These, whether they will or no, are being inexorably educated. What is to be taught of doctrine and of the Scripture is that which Origen preaches and comments upon. It has been convincingly insinuated that his homiletical method for justifying the severity of Providence to men springs from consciously pedagogical assumptions. The homily on Jer. 12:3 points out that God no more chastises for the joy of punishing than does the master of a slave or the father of a son; rather, this educator-God, in leading the erring ones from sin, employs stern correctives only where the Word fails.

The divine " cure of souls " is, truly, a " school of souls," even as Christ the Lord is " Master of souls." Origen presses this instructional and reclamatory element to its logical end. Heretics will be subjected to redeeming chastisements. The education of souls is one of stages — seven, in fact, as he sets forth in his homily on Jer. 7:2. Some there are who have their eyes opened with the completion of the first stage. Others prove still refractory to the divine preceptor with the conclusion of the seventh. What can be done then is not discussed in this context, though the famous passages in the *Principles* show how strong was Origen's educator-faith in God's power, ultimately, to enlighten all minds and hearts unto salvation.

A substantial section of Tollinton's translations drawn from Origen's commentaries and homilies is most appropriately entitled " The Teacher and His Task." Virtually all these are concerned with one central thesis: namely, that the teaching and preaching of the Word is the basic response on the Christian leader's part to the divine illumination. So the Christian scribe, the true disciple of the Kingdom of Heaven, is like the man who is a householder bringing forth from his treasure chest things new and old. " Therefore should we endeavour by every means to gather together in our heart, through giving heed to reading, to exhortation, to teaching " both the new oracles of the Gospels and apostles and " the old oracles of the Law."

Jesus himself is the true householder " who brings forth from his treasure at the season of instruction things new, . . . and old." He may enrich the scribe who has been made a disciple to the Kingdom of Heaven and make him like unto himself. " At last the disciple will become as his master." From this master there proceed things new, the gospel teaching, and things old, " the comparison of sayings taken from the Law and the Prophets, of which examples may be found in the Gospels."

In the homily on Jeremiah, section 14:1–5, Origen's preoccupation is with the teacher-physician's difficulty in ministering to recalcitrant patients of the spirit. The manner in which preachers, truly teaching the Word, may be helped by their hearers is much in his mind. Just as a prophetic speaker is helped by willing hearers, so the teacher " by his very teaching is helped in his teaching and his studies through the intelligence of his pupil. Lecturers become more competent in the very instruction they impart, when their hearers are intelligent and do not accept their words right off, but criticise them and ask questions and examine the meaning of the language used." The head of the catechetical school, the inquirer of the cosmos, the synthesizer of universal meanings, is here teaching and preaching.

That Origen was not always conscious of the exact demarcation line separating his teaching from his preaching is attestation to a Christian dilemma some of us may deplore. Nevertheless, Christian history records this peril as having certain edifying aspects as well. Important as it undoubtedly is that the preaching and teaching functions be not undiscriminatingly equated, it is as surely imperative that the contributions of each be properly capitalized by the other on occasion.

The Historical Alliance of Teaching and Preaching

It is clear that from a very early date the ministries of preaching and teaching frequently proceed in practically inseparable alliance; even as, on occasion, they assume sharply differentiated obligations. That bishops, as well as priests and other assistants episcopally designated, had at the same time the duties of preaching and teaching often means simply this: one who preached was really teaching Christian doctrine; one who taught might be preaching in the truest sense. That in the ancient Church, as later, one designated as a teacher might not be in orders, or authorized to preach publicly, goes without saying. As Elliott-Binns says, in *The Beginnings of Western Christendom*, " Doubtless, teaching was part of the Church's activities from the very earliest days, and those who had the necessary gifts would take their share in it." Of course, not all were so qualified. Apostolic recognition probably inhered in the office. With no clearly defined functions at first, the teacher most frequently emerges in the Early Church as an instructor of baptismal candidates and others already Christian. In North Africa, for instance, some presbyters were apparently set apart for teaching services. But teachers were not always clergy. Certain Early Church manuals show both ecclesiasts and laymen joining in this work; and laying hands upon, and praying for, the catechumens instructed.

That the bishop, who was increasingly recognized as the guardian of preaching prerogatives, became also the custodian of properly taught doctrine is reflected fairly soon in ecclesiastical literature. Let it be remembered, however, that the functions involved were frequently so nearly identical as to give rise to an almost embarrassingly interchangeable terminology in much of the Church's literary usage.

As already noted in Chrysostom's homilies, one thus trained in the classics and steeped in the Christian faith consistently preached the gospel he taught and taught the good news he evangelized. For instance, his eleventh homily on Saint John takes the opportunity to instruct those under his preaching ministry as to the educational procedures they should adopt at home in order to appropriate the word preached in church. He specifically anticipates home reading in the Scriptures as the minimal preparation by his parishioners for the reception of the preached message.

In the fourth book of his treatise *On the Priesthood,* a passage dealing specifically with the gravity and opportunity of the preacher's task, Chrysostom deals at length with that teaching, which is, at times, obviously preaching. He also recognizes differentiations between these closely allied Christian arts. What is clearly evident is his conviction that, although a teacher may not necessarily have a public preaching function, a preacher cannot fail to teach Christian doctrine and still be a preacher. And he would certainly make provision for harvesting the teacher's work in the storehouse of his preaching colleague.

As for the intellectual discipline incumbent upon the public preacher, John Chrysostom enumerates an icily comforting doctrine: the better preacher a man becomes, the harder he needs to study. Those hearing the public preacher customarily refuse his ministrations as a teacher, preferring for themselves a role like that of onlookers at the public games to that of learners in the Christian way. If, in moving his listeners from the critic's seat to the mourner's bench, he skirts sheer abuse and adulation alike, for the glory of God alone, he will need study in plenty. Furthermore, from such application will come the man who can " undertake the strain of teaching " without regard to the " good opinion of the outside world "; always " laboring at his sermons so that he may please God "; content with his consciousness " of arranging and ordering his teaching " to that end.

Moreover, a man so companionably lodged as Chrysostom in a preaching-teaching environment would be the logical one to set his hearers to teaching and preaching with their very lives. His would be the ideal plea that the Christ-follower " show the Greeks " how much they missed in not being Christians. So too his teacher's analysis and rejection, in advance, of Christian pretexts for not " kindling the Lord's fire " would make the nominal churchman's excuses obsolete before they were fully thought out, much less uttered.

As for the manner in which an erstwhile monk and full-time bishop preached and taught, Basil of Caesarea is an interesting example. Even learned clergymen today frequently express surprise that the Middle Ages were so taken with Basil's homilies on the Creation. Yet some of these same brethren are always scrambling, with considerably more haste and less intellectual dignity than he, to show that religion can still hold up its head in a world of science. It may be suspected, however, that people tire less, the ages through, of a preacher like Basil, who has a message both before and after current science has issued its

manifestoes, than they do of one who is always announcing that
it is perfectly safe to believe religious truths once more, now
that science has spoken. Perhaps few would care to go surety
for Basil's brand of molecular physics and atomic fission. Just
the same, one may at least rejoice that here was an intelligent
and well-educated preacher who felt it necessary to teach
Christian truths in relation to a world of physical phenomena
and ultimate realities.

We may defer for a time the extended consideration of Augustine's *On Christian Doctrine,* a treatise par excellence on
the fruitful union of teaching and preaching as they involve
the interpretation of the Scriptures and the functions of public
exhortation.

Without doubt, the edifying eighth-century homilies of the
Venerable Bede are bent especially upon inculcating Christian
teaching. For him, the fishermen of Luke 5:2 " are the teachers
of the Church, who gather us together in the net of faith and
lift us up out of the depths into the light, like fish upon the
shore, and thus bring us to the land of the living. Like the nets
of the fishers are the discourses of the preachers, which enmesh
those whom they receive in faith " (16:104–105).

Anselm, the eleventh-century scholastic, preaching upon
Peter's coming " *down out of the ship, and* [walking] *on the
water to go to Jesus,*" explains: " This has been fulfilled, and
still is fulfilling; when holy preachers are sent forth to heathen
nations. For Peter comes down out of the ship as often as any
holy doctor descends from the bosom of the Church, his
Mother, where he has been educated, and goes with pious con-
descension to them that are without, that he may show them
the way of salvation." Peter, then, " typifies the order of
preachers " (25:136–137).

Bernard of Clairvaux, who has sometimes been chided for a
less-than-enthusiastic reception of the schools, is concerned for

true learning and good conversation of life on the part of every pastor, " for how can one who is ignorant conduct the Lord's flocks to the sweet pastures of the Divine oracles? " Along with a life that speaks for God, there must be a nourishing of the faithful by the abundance of doctrine.

The further solicitude for preaching that shall be good teaching — that is, fundamentally, the inculcation of true doctrine — is a veritable commonplace with later medieval preachers. It may be well, therefore, to bring into clearer perspective selected aspects of the preaching-teaching function as it is represented by typical spokesmen.

PREACHING THE OFFICIAL TEACHING OF THE CHURCH

It should prove instructive to look at a few leaders who regard preaching as the instrument for setting forth, officially, the credal and moral teachings of the Church. Augustine has left us just such a sermon on " The Tradition [or Handing Down] of the Creed." To his listeners he explains why the Creed is called the Symbol. " The time has come for you to receive the Creed which contains in few words all which you believe for your eternal salvation. We rightly call it the Symbol, from the analogy of another use of the word — for merchants have a symbol or sign which they use among themselves to keep the members of their association faithful to their agreement. And you are members of a spiritual association, seeking, like merchants, the *pearl of great price*. . . . This pearl is love, which *is poured forth in* [your] *hearts by the Holy Ghost who is given to* [you]. . . . Such love is attained through the faith which is contained in this Symbol." There follow, then, the articles of that faith as it embraces the distinctiveness, in inseparable unity, of Father, Son, and Holy Spirit. And Augustine concludes: " I have preached to you this short sermon on the whole Creed, as is required. In that Creed you know that all

I have said in this sermon is contained in few words. These words you must not write down in any way in order to preserve them. Learn them by hearing them. . . . This, then, is the Creed. Its substance is already known to you through the Scriptures and the preaching of the Church. But this brief form must be steadfastly held and upheld by the faithful" (13:87–90).

The ninth-century emperor, Charles the Great, under the strong impulse of Augustinian ideals, planned a sweeping reorganization of church life within his realm. With a freedom that amounts at times to virtual arrogance, he writes popes, bishops, and other churchmen concerning their duties within his empire. These letters, like his laws, have to do primarily with the elevation, not so much of the purely cultural level, as of the Christian character and deportment of his people. Convinced, as he is, that a Christian king may speak with impunity concerning the spiritual as well as the temporal necessities of his day, Charlemagne directs a campaign against ignorance and inertia among the priests, first, and, consequently, within the parishes that they serve. Thus, he writes bishops of high standing with great frankness concerning the defective celebration of the cult and the inadequate proclamation of the Christian gospel in their dioceses. He declares that preaching to the people must be given a central place in order that ordinary morality may be fostered and that the worship of God may be properly reinforced.

Since the emperor proposes to have his society operating on a Christian basis, he holds it perfectly within his rights to dispose his clerical forces to the best advantage and to give them training of a sweeping kind within the everyday affairs of life. Whether in concert with episcopal advisers, or on the basis of his own independent judgment, he issues mandates for the instruction of the priesthood. The questions to be asked, then, upon the occasion of their ordination, range over the field of their knowledge of the Catholic principles of doctrine, the proper order of the Mass, the Gospels as they are conceived in his age, the homilies from the patristic era that are available for guidance in Scriptural exposition, and the approved means of carrying on parish life. Needless to say, there were those who disagreed with Charlemagne as to the objectives and methods of securing such reform. But they could hardly oppose his insistence upon reform itself; and they more frequently supported his emphasis on preaching and teaching as a proper instrument of Christian development than they resisted it. The general level of church life was at such a low ebb that almost any improvement would be welcome. Charlemagne did not think it possible to effect sweeping changes overnight. He was thoroughly convinced, however, that attention to the simple fundamentals of the Christian faith, once incorporated in the clerical consciousness, would be bound to show results among the people, in due course of time. In this, he was not wholly wrong.

The well-schooled and reform-minded pontiff Innocent III stated in a sermon of his own the need for the careful preacher who would " compose his sermon with a variety of material and many different authorities so that he speaks now of virtues, now of faults; sometimes of rewards, again of penalties, somewhat of mercy, and somewhat of justice; now simply, now subtly; using history, then allegory; speaking now literally, now figuratively; citing authorities and giving arguments; employing metaphors and illustrations — so that *each point takes its place fitly set forth* " (34:179). This last member of the quotation, by the way, is documented by the pope to Horace. Such a preacher, employing the best procedure of the schools and stressing the life-giving doctrines of the Church, would edify all whom he thus taught.

The third council of the Lateran in 1179 had sought to sub-
sidize instruction for clerics and poor students in every ca-
thedral church. Thus, also, the Fourth Lateran of 1215, so dear
to Innocent's heart, reiterated the earlier teaching provision
and associated with it a new canon (10) on preaching. This
reads in part: " Among other things that pertain to the salvation of the Christian people, the food of the word of God is
above all necessary. . . . It often happens that bishops, on account of their manifold duties or bodily infirmities, or because
of hostile invasions or other reasons, to say nothing of lack of
learning, which must be absolutely condemned in them and is
not to be tolerated in the future, are themselves unable to
minister the word of God to the people, especially in large and
widespread dioceses. Wherefore we decree that bishops provide
suitable men, powerful in work and word, to exercise with fruitful result the office of preaching; who in place of the bishops,
since these cannot do it, diligently visiting the people committed to them, may instruct them by word and example."

Peter of Blois, who died at the beginning of the thirteenth
century, was well-known and beloved throughout a wide circle
of acquaintances. He too spared no one in declaring the unique
obligations of the ministry for clear Christian teaching and re-
sponsible doctrine. Not only in his sermons, which were widely
heard and read in his day, but also in his famous epistles, he
directed attention to the preacher's responsibility for reform.
In his letters which are, in a sense, a veritable preaching manual, he writes to newly elevated bishops concerning their duties.
In paragraph after paragraph, he passes by the opportunity to
congratulate them on their new eminence so that he may warn
them about temptations of pride. One passage will suffice to
illustrate many of a similar sort. Speaking to a well-known
bishop-elect, he reminds him that the *episcopos* is called to
such a duty, not as an opportunity for self-aggrandizement and

the entrenchment of avaricious relatives, but for the salvation of God's people. This letter and others like it are a growing commentary on the necessity of fleeing clerical acquisitiveness and seeking new fields of service to sinful humanity. Obviously a bishop is liable, not only for his own studies and spiritual growth, but also for the direction of other ministers who, together with him, will be the shepherds of Christian flocks. Such sermons as remain from him indicate that he could adapt his message to the ecclesiastical aristocracy and country audiences, alike.

Manuals on Preaching

A significant device for implanting sound doctrine through revived homiletics was the manual for teaching the art of preaching. The fullest development of these homiletic handbooks was associated with the revival of preaching from the eleventh century onward — particularly among the mendicants.

Several works, however, like Augustine's *On Christian Doctrine,* had laid the groundwork in the earlier periods for much more technical aids to later sermon production and delivery. The work known as *Concerning Christian Teaching,* or *On Christian Doctrine,* has a particularly close relationship to the ministerial art throughout the Christian ages. The first three books constitute the first major division of the work and have to do with what the author calls the discovery of the true sense of Scripture. These first three books, then, canvass at length the many intricate problems associated with Scriptural exegesis and interpretation — actually hermeneutics.

The real bearing of the treatise for the problem of preaching, or homiletics, however, is found in the fourth, and last, book. It is particularly directed toward the means of interpreting the Scriptures through the rhetorical art. To be sure, Augustine does not contemplate a treatise on rhetoric in and of itself. There are books in plenty on that subject which his readers may consult if they wish.

Nonetheless, Chapter 2 does contend for the usefulness of rhetoric in its proper place where a Christian teacher is concerned. Incidentally, the term " teacher " is in this connection well-nigh synonymous with that of " preacher," inasmuch as the teaching of the Scriptures here takes on the character of the preacher's art. " Since, then, the faculty of eloquence is available for both sides, and is of very great service in the enforcing either of wrong or right, why do not good men study to engage it on the side of truth, when bad men use it to obtain the triumph of wicked and worthless causes, and to further injustice and error? "

After a consideration of the manner in which rhetoric may be so employed (Chapter 3) our author takes up in greater detail the duty of the Christian teacher (Chapter 4). Although Augustine treats of this issue in a brief introductory paragraph, he does not regard it as a simple one. After all, the interpreter and teacher of Holy Scripture is " the defender of the true faith and the opponent of error." He has the obligation not only of teaching what is right but of refuting what is erroneous. In performing this task he must be prepared to " conciliate the hostile, to rouse the careless, and to tell the ignorant both what is occurring at present and what is probable in the future." Anticipating also the matter of different hearers and different occasions, he lays down an introductory program for meeting the various situations. As need arises, people must be aroused, informed, instructed on difficult points, and sufficiently moved in the emotions to secure ultimate action.

In Chapters 5, 6, and 7 there is a demonstration of the necessary balancing of eloquence and wisdom. The holy authors are demonstrably rich in their combination of these qualities.

Augustine is very clearly producing a pattern here that is to become noteworthy throughout the Middle Ages: that is, however much precedence should be accorded the matter and content of preaching, no little significance attaches to the form, style, delivery, and general effectiveness of expression. It is not strange that many writers on the art of preaching should return periodically to this Augustinian prototype.

One is reminded in Chapter 8 that there is no virtue in following the sacred writers in such slavish fashion as to obscure every point for the reader that they have left unclear. Naturally, the Christian teacher ought first of all to make himself understood.

Chapters 9 and 10 take up such practical affairs as how, and with whom, difficult passages are to be discussed; and the necessity for clear style. In Chapter 11 a premium is placed upon clarity of speech which, however, does not necessarily entail infelicitous expression. The teaching art aims always to bring lucidity out of obscurity. But all possible grace of style that may be brought to bear enhances the interest and susceptibility of the hearer. Augustine observes that " as there is a certain analogy between learning and eating, the very food without which it is impossible to live must be flavoured to meet the tastes of the majority."

The chapters immediately following would be hard to surpass for their cogency and enduring usefulness to the student of the preaching art. The regularity with which subsequent masters return to Augustine for instruction and inspiration is sufficient tribute in this connection. When, in Chapter 12, Augustine quotes Cicero, somewhat inexactly, as to the ends of public speech, he is not failing to keep the distinctively Christian objective in mind. " ' An eloquent man must speak so as to teach, to delight, and to persuade. . . . To teach is a necessity, to delight is a beauty, to persuade is a triumph.' " Teaching, "which is a matter of necessity, depends on what we say; the other two [that is, delighting and persuading] on the way we say it." Once having achieved understanding, he who wishes to delight or persuade his hearer, as well, may quite logically concern himself with the importance attached to the style of speaking. Furthermore, just "as the hearer must be pleased in order to secure his attention, so he must be persuaded in order to move him to action." There are people who know what is being said and who enjoy hearing it. Still, they may not derive any real profit from it. What real advantage comes to a man who "both confesses the truth and praises the eloquence, if he does not yield his consent, when it is only for the sake of securing his consent that the speaker in urging the truth gives careful attention to what he says?" (Chapter 13). If mere believing or knowing these truths is sufficient, "to give one's assent implies nothing more than to confess that they are true." The Christian orator who wishes to win his chief objective must not only use instruction to secure a proper disposition of his auditor; he must not only please to such an extent that he will captivate his listener; he must, even more, touch the inner qualities of mind and will which lead to whole-souled commitment.

As Chapter 14 insists, beauty of diction ought to be in keeping with the content treated. It is all too easy to make a great rhetorical display of matter that is singularly unimportant. Floridity is scarcely ever a virtue; though on occasion the preacher may find it useful to relieve a style that seems unduly chastened and severe.

Chapter 15 admonishes the Christian teacher to pray before preaching. Here again the Augustinian emphasis is such as to be repeated almost endlessly in subsequent manuals. "And when the hour is come that he must speak, he ought, before he opens his mouth, to lift up his thirsty soul to God, to drink in what he is about to pour forth, and to be himself filled with what he is about to distribute. For, as in regard to every matter of faith and love there are many things that may be said, and many ways of saying them, who knows what is expedient at a given moment for us to say, or to be heard saying, except God who knows the hearts of all? " Having mastered all possible sources of information before the time of preaching, the minister should then be free to receive the infilling of the divine spirit. In this sense, and not through any disparagement of rational preparation, the preacher may " take no thought how or what [he] shall speak." Chapter 16, entitled " Human Directions Not to Be Despised, Though God Makes the True Teacher," is little more than a continuation of this same subject.

Chapter 17 has as its burden of Ciceronian admonition the proper balancing of style in terms of more and less weighty subjects: " ' He, then, shall be eloquent, who can say little things in a subdued style, in order to give instruction, moderate things in a temperate style, in order to give pleasure, and great things in a majestic style, in order to sway the mind.' "

Chapters 18 to 26 are really amplifications of the foregoing principles. Augustine brings from the Holy Scripture examples of simplicity in style which recall, not only his acquaintance with the sacred text, but also his identification with the people to whom he habitually preaches. The Doctors of the Church are relied upon for their fair portion of illustration. Ambrose, who had meant so much in Augustine's own personal experience, together with Cyprian and others, serves to enhance the impressions that Augustine would create. Appropriateness, proper regard to the demands of the occasion, together with a sensible change of pace, are all called for.

Nothing is more important than the emphasis of Chapters 27 to 29. Here it is insisted that if a man is to speak with maximum effectiveness his life must preach a message in harmony with his words. It is of course conceivable that some good things could be learned from a bad man. But it is much more apparent how increasingly fruitful are the results obtained by those whose practice is in accordance with their preaching.

Chapter 29 emphasizes a point that has been exploited by a few courageous souls with pardonable caution, namely, that " it is permissible for a preacher to deliver to the people what has been written by a more eloquent man than himself."

Chapter 30 reverts once more to the all-important prayer by which a preacher should commence his discourse. Whether a man proposes to preach in his own person, or to secure a reading to the people of another's sermons, he ought in any case to make provisions for proper prayer. One ought to pray God " to put into his mouth a suitable discourse."

Gregory the Great, in his *Pastoral Rule,* is only indirectly, yet significantly, concerned with preaching method. His work is utilized by Charlemagne and Alfred in their programs of church instruction which are calculated to raise the general level of preaching and teaching. Gregory's manual must be properly appreciated for its short but pointed remarks on the purpose, varied objectives, and multiple audience-situations of the Christian preacher. There is in his writing an admittedly large debt to Gregory Nazianzen, Chrysostom, and Ambrose. Gregory is, in turn, utilized widely by myriads of less distinguished, as well as some very able, churchmen.

Gregory's exposition on I Kings is almost a preaching manual in itself. This work calls for a high premium on preaching and teaching as virtually identical functions. After all, preachers have a terrifying answerability to God for the proclamation of the Scripture. Like their Master, preachers must rise above all carnality and popular suasion; knowing that if, by the prosecution of knowledge, they do not come to the height of the Scriptures, they shall surely not ascend to the hill of the Lord.

A remarkably astute delineation of preacher-teacher problems is evidenced in a recently translated sermon of Gregory. At the risk of all-round dissatisfaction and inadequate representation we may quote a few topic sentences from various paragraphs on the preacher who is a genuine teacher; or, more properly, the teaching-preacher. The pastor-teacher " ought to consider what he should say, and to whom, and when, and how, and how much." *To whom* — " because often the word of rebuke which one person will accept, another will not." *When* — " because often, if the rebuke is postponed, it afterward is readily received. But sometimes it loses force, if one misses the time at which it should have been given." *How* — " for often the words which recall one man to salvation wound another." *How much* — " lest we prolong the word of exhortation or rebuke too far for the one who is not able to bear much, and thus bring our hearer to boredom " (15:98–99). Prolixity, of course, entails its own peculiar problems at all times.

With a few exceptions not germane to our present discussion, careful expositions of the theory and practice of preaching are well-nigh absent from the eighth to the twelfth century. Those of the twelfth reflect the trends of scholastically oriented, more systematically constructed sermons. The invaluable preaching *Summas* of De Nogent and De Lille, which we cannot analyze here, give way to a thirteenth-century series of manuals distinctively suited to the homiletics of the Franciscan and Dominican apostolates.

These and their later adaptations stress sermon objectives, content, structural form, preparation, and delivery. Types of hearers and the varieties of circumstances confronting the preacher are traditionally important parts of the manuals. The internal structure of the sermon is meticulously handled according to theme, protheme, divisions or distinctions and their proper subheadings, and, finally, development and expansion. *Exempla*, that is, illustrations, and their uses almost never fail of a large share of attention. Authorities and citations from various sources prove to be much more relevant, classically, and far more richly pertinent, Biblically, than is usually supposed. The use and interpretation of Scripture raise a series of questions, involving not only the four senses, but also the whole content and form of the Christian tradition. Matters of vernacular language and the preacher's auditory are not entirely neglected, though they are seldom dealt with in a way satisfactory to us. Problems of style, voice, pace, and gestures are soberly, although not excessively, considered. Beginner's advice and special admonitions for greater effectiveness are often treated in the sanest possible fashion.

From the comprehensive preaching manual of a fourteenth-century English Dominican, a few pertinent teaching suggestions are here repeated in abbreviated paraphrase. Says Thomas Waleys in effect: Let the preacher beware of subtracting from his effectiveness by harboring cherished personal sins. The praise of God and edification of neighbor, not ostentation, are the ends of his ministry. Proper modesty in deportment and gesture is indispensable. Good sense says: Be neither an immobile statue nor an animated caricature. Watch your language and capitalize good speech methods. An experienced preacher speaks and is warmly received. Another uses almost the same words and gets nowhere. Why? Reputation counts, of course, but not entirely. It's partly a matter of speech manners and the effective exploitation of language.

The manner of speech is scarcely less significant than its content. Speak not too loudly or too softly. Shout and offend the refined. Speak too low and fail to be heard. Now shouting, now whispering, you offend all. Clamor to the heavens and repel those nearest you. Speak too low and the distant auditors think you have secrets with a few. Discipline your delivery as to proper velocity, distinctness, and moderate pauses.

Don't foster the suspicion that you are preaching another's sermon and have not had time to assimilate it yourself. Don't recite like a child. Take care not to bombard people with words that have no meaning for them. Following Paul's advice, prefer five words with understanding to ten thousand in tongues. Ponder your words. If you don't, how can your hearers? Cultivate stylistic clarity; avoid prolixity and redundancy. Give digests, sometimes, rather than extensive quotations.

Speak to the heart, not just the ears, of Jerusalem. Avoid vain display and affectation. Strive to please God, not men. Be careful of saying anything about those, especially, who are absent; avoid preaching against anyone unless the total welfare of church and people, or the culprit's own spiritual needs, demands it. When necessary, speak fearlessly. Speak the truth without dissimulation. Proclaim the Word of God with faithfulness.

Let inexperienced preachers try out voice and gestures before speaking; on trees and stones, preferably. Get your friends to criticize you. Watch your enunciation and voice timbre. Don't despair! Keep on practicing.

These preaching aids — *artes praedicandi* as they were called — constituted the beginning, not the conclusion, of the whole matter of preaching. But help they did. And they would still help, if we studied them.

Preaching and Teaching in the School of Christ

Such affinities between Christian preaching and teaching had another and more intimate side, however. Origen, Bonaventura, Robert de Sorbon, and many others studied, preached, and taught to the glory of God. As they did so, they sustained a sense of close Master-and-student relationship. This concerned their academic preparation for public and private teaching. It involved, also, their own common studentship in their divine Lord and Master's school.

Preaching on the illuminating, instructional versatility of Christ and his Church, Origen says of the human spirit: " The higher and the further it goes in its approach to Christ, the more nearly it exposes itself to the glory of His light, the more finely and splendidly is it illuminated by His radiance. . . . And if a man be even so advanced as to be able to go up with Him to the mount, as Peter and James and John, he shall have the illumination not only of the light of Christ but even of the very Father's voice " (4:51).

Over one thousand years later, Bonaventura — the Franciscan teacher, preacher, and mystic — employs the magisterial analogy. He apostrophizes in a sermon, " Be Ye Merciful," the compassion the Lord has on us " as a master upon his disciple. . . . In two ways the Master takes pity on his disciple: he illuminates his mind and comforts him with his affection. Thus God reveals marvelous visions to those who are in his school, and fills them with ineffable consolation. . . . Thus the merciful man, especially the prelate of the Church, ought compassionately to teach his subordinates, so that he may increase the fruits of their spirits and in the future receive a hundredfold from God " (41:221, 223).

Mixing humor and pathos, and holding out blame and blessing, Robert de Sorbon in the thirteenth century produced a sermon upon the similarity of student examinations at the University of Paris with the grand finals at the Judgment Day. It is a remarkable airing of Christian responsibility as it should be entertained by preachers and teachers, whether for student preparation or soul salvation. Reminiscing upon the occasionally loose methods of the human teacher, Sorbon recalls how some examiners are content if a student struggles reasonably well through a portion of the book he is being asked to master. But the great Examiner-Judge will make the candidate read every word of the whole book of conscience as it affects both his personal and social responsibility before he passes him to a licentiate in heavenly glory.

Yet another scholar, teacher, and preacher — though denied in the main the popular ministry he so yearned for — dignified prayerfully the response of the human to the divine Master. Nicholas of Cusa rejoices thus: " I render Thee thanks, Jesu, that by Thy light I have come thus far. In Thy light I see the light of my life. I see how Thou, the Word, infusest life into all believers, and makest perfect all that love Thee. What teaching, good Jesu, was ever briefer and more effectual than Thine? Thou persuadest us but to believe, Thou biddest us but to love. What is easier than to believe in God? What is sweeter than to love Him? How pleasant is Thy yoke, how light is Thy burden, Thou one and only Teacher! To them that obey this teaching Thou dost promise all their desires, for Thou requirest naught difficult to a believer, and naught that a lover can refuse. Such are the promises that Thou makest unto Thy disciples, and they are entirely true, for Thou art the truth, who canst promise naught but truth. Nay more, 'tis naught other than Thyself that Thou dost promise, who art the perfection of all that may be made perfect. To Thee be praise, to Thee be glory, to Thee the rendering of thanks through endless ages! Amen."

Teachers and preachers of the pre-Reformation period did not rise uniformly to such heights any more than those of our own day. But among them were Wulfstans — to set ablaze, not only the private conscience, but also the collective will for better response to God's plan among men. So too there were men like Peter of Blois to preach the priceless teaching of

Christian fear leading to Godly love. And he held forth, likewise, on the worm that dies not in the cancerous vitals of an unworthy priest. There, too, was Jacques de Vitry, gospel campaigner and shrewd psychologist, who knew how to sympathize with laborers victimized by their taskmasters; just as he was quick to remind these same employees how they could, and did, cheat their employers.

Teaching Private and Public Responsibility

On the list of preachers teaching moral and spiritual duties as they affected private and public responsibility Berthold of Regensburg cannot be left out. Fearlessly, he pays his gospel respects to the various categories of vocational and professional tricksters. Hear him in his scarcely academic indictment of workers in " clothing, silks, or wool or fur, shoes or gloves or girdles." " Nowadays," he complains, " no man can find a good hat for thy falsehood; the rain will pour down through the brim into his bosom. Even such deceit is there in shoes, in furs, in curriers' work; one man sells an old skin for a new, and how manifold are your deceits no man knoweth so well as thou and thy master the devil. Why should I come here to teach thee frauds? Thou knowest enough thyself " (38:206).

As for ill-prepared medics — veritable quacks — he pooh-poohs their isolated successes as a series of lucky accidents. They have accidents enough of the unlucky variety. To them he says: " We have murderers enough without thee, to slay honest folk. Deal with thy wounds for the present, and practise the rest until thou be past master. Whether they be children or old folk, thou hast much need of good art before thou canst well cut them for the stone " (38:209).

Time prevents our telling now how he pleaded with vain women not to slam the Kingdom of Heaven's door shut in their own faces with their passion for flounces and fancy hairdos,

their " crimple-crispings here " and their " christy-crosties
there." Nor is it meet that we retail his advice to the husband
to be, not a mouse, but a man, and to tear off that veil from
his wife's head " even though four or ten hairs should come
away with it, and cast it into the fire! " It is not right that we
should listen to him — certainly not with some nostalgic smile
— as he explains how man may be, once more, what we know
he has never been, i.e., " woman's lord and master " (39:213).
Even God's prophet must be permitted an occasional moment
of phantasy.

To Bernardine of Siena — canon lawyer, teacher, and
preacher to the people — we must return later. But he also
used the preaching office for teaching the Christian his routine
duties — to church, school, and civic community. Unto the
officeholder he says: " Be not puffed up! Hast thou an office?
Yes. O hold not thy head so high, lest thou knock it against
something " (55:277). In the analysis of contemporary social
issues and hardheaded Christian correctives he has few peers.

Teaching and preaching, then, belonged together in the Great
Tradition. Fitting it is, therefore, that Michel Menot, contemporary of Luther's emergence, should take for his text Isa.
58:1: " Cry, cease not, lift up thy voice like a trumpet "; and
then proceed to teach how to preach, by preaching. Thus he
begins: " It is Isaiah who, today, marks out for us the pattern
to be followed in preaching. . . . What then is this pattern?
We are told," he says, " what it is and ought to be ":

> *Ardor in exhortation*
> *Authority in instruction*
> *Austerity in condemnation.*

As to ardor: " The first requirement for preaching is that the
preacher must speak, not merely from his mouth, but also from
his heart. Therefore, holy preaching is not like a musical per-

formance given solely to refresh the audience. The worldly to-day are still saying: *Speak unto us pleasant things,* . . . and we will hear you. . . . Truly, courage and a sincere heart are required to exhort a sinful people."

And what of authority in instruction? " The preachers and priests today are successors to the office of the apostles, the proclaiming of the word of God. . . . Therefore, as the Lord said to the apostles, *go . . . and preach*."

What, at last, of austerity in condemnation? " Wide is the difference between the voice of the preacher and the piping of the shepherd which serves only to make the goats leap. For when duty requires the preacher to attack sin. . . , his voice is like the voice of a trumpet, sounding and striking the heart " (60:301–305).

Bringing to life these brief excerpts are seven printed pages, in modern equivalent, of the teacher's analysis and the preacher's platform. Here, as always, preaching and teaching press forward, shoulder to shoulder. Co-operatively, they exercise their distinctive gifts in the glorious prosecution of the one Christian ministry.

Chapter Three

PREACHING AND THE MINISTRY
TO THE COMMON LIFE

PREACHING is the ministry to the common life. This is the credo of the Lord's spokesmen who are sent in service to that community of mingled despair and ecstasy which, with all its shared mortality, comprises the human race.

Preaching means nothing if it does not bring "Word and worship" into the lives of the people; if it does not summon them to hear the gospel and to bow before the eternal. Jesus prayed frequently — often alone — but he also heard the people's cry and responded to it. "That is why I came out here," he said. He preached throughout Galilee, healing minds, souls, and bodies. Lepers came to him. People sensed in him a companion's regard, a more than "manly" concern. He left town for country, and "people came to him from every quarter." He went to the synagogue; he read and spoke there of his kinship with the disinherited and oppressed. He yearned to join his people in Temple service, but he bridled at the way in which sinning, savable humanity was being defrauded and victimized.

The apostles in Acts 6:1–5 were right in putting common prayers and shared word before social service as such. But they were impelled by this very experience to a course of action inescapable for worshiping, witnessing Christians: they began providing for widows, orphans, and others in need.

In all Christian history nothing has been more spiritually de-
structive than keeping the people and God apart. This dire
separation has often been accentuated, if not initiated, by
preaching that is alien in thought or language, lazy in preparation or delivery, undisciplined in content or form, puerile in
conception or expression, and feeble in downsweep and up-
thrust. One may survey historically the ancient Church, medieval Christendom, the Protestant era, and our own modern,
sophisticated age. Throughout these successive periods nothing
has proved so disappointing on many occasions, and so explo-
sive on others, as preaching to the people: preaching to them
God's stern, loving, numbing, exhilarating, and reconciling
Word.

The preaching function and community activities have their
differentiating as well as their affiliating experiences. People
have a right to congregate on occasions supposedly immune
to ministerial infiltration. The retreat of a little girl, age three
and three quarters, who failed at the last moment to attend a
long-anticipated missionary meeting at her mother's house, un-
derlines this reminder. Having repelled sadly, but firmly, her
mother's every effort to lure her downstairs, where she was
accustomed to assist in serving tea, she confided to her grand-
mother the cause of her perturbation. She had just learned that
the minister was to be in attendance. " And you know," she
said with a sigh, " I just can't take a chance on going down
there and getting baptized." The scholar Bede had, on one occasion, lent the prestige of his venerability to the tartness of a
strikingly similar observation: " Not every time is suitable for
teaching, but sometimes the teacher ought to engage in preaching, and sometimes he ought to attend to his own concerns "
(cf. 16:105).

But if the people have to guard against pastoral ubiquity,
the preacher, for his part, has to defend places and seasons of

prophetic privacy against the extroversions of the populace.
He has to beware of becoming merely a community man; of
constituting in himself the people's vibrating harp; of being
the flattering mirror of their gregarious selves. Preachers are
not the Lord's ministers plenipotentiary, his jovial greeters, to
each elite human gathering that holds the "keys to the city"
for the day. As a sixteenth-century preacher brusquely observed, there is a vast difference between the shepherd's piping to frisky goats and the prophet's thundering with awesome
tuba voice. Social joys are the people's right. But the preacher
who feels no responsibility to declare God's plan of eternal
beatitude, and how it affects our corporate existence today, is
a hater of man's delight.

Preaching is for the people. They need it as bewildered, be-
nighted travelers need a way, a light, and a voice. It is the
people that the Lord wants saved. It is to them that prophets
are sent. They are the ones that God's voice must reach, his
truth enlighten, his terms set free.

And these same people must be confronted in their collective existence, not only in their solitary musings. They must
be shocked into life and deprived of their self-styled right of
defeating the Lord's love, each in his own way. Furthermore,
this life of the people is the life of us all. None has any priority
of righteousness, in himself, over those to whom he preaches.
But the blood of everyone to whom he speaks not, or to whom
he rumbles on in soothing platitudes, is already on his own
head.

Naturally, when the people receive the gospel they make of
the preacher's life a thing of misery and — paradoxically but
no less truly — a joy forever. People, and that includes the
preaching-teaching profession, attack the preacher who speaks
boldly, and the one who does not. They refuse, scorn, deride,
willfully misinterpret, villify — and finally capitulate to the

good news and its announcers. Those who preach to the common life must speak plainly, out of depths not always left uncovered. They must use language as bruising as the prophets', and as gentle as parenthood's dream for its young. They must suit message to hearer, and discipline according to God's, not their own, wisdom.

It was in this way that Augustine preached visiting prelates from behind convenient posts. As they peeked out to get a look at him, he transfixed them with gospel words. Thus Bernard of Clairvaux blazed through popular gatherings and concourses of truculent princes, not to mention assemblages of newly elevated churchlings and convocations of sleepy monastics. Similarly, Jacques de Vitry riveted the interest of farm laborers with an unforgettably illustrated message before they had time to turn their backs upon him. So, too, Meister Eckhart dropped people's jaws and dried up their tongues so that they forgot to misunderstand what he meant. These preachers, like Gregory Nazianzen, spurned " ecclesiastical ventriloquism " and visceral bombast as they charged their voices with God's own power. They sat in no ecclesiastical laps and they scorned being artful, wooden scavengers from other men's lips. Actually, they put into lively homiletic play a vocabulary often reminiscent of the Master's own.

Always, whether in school or in the pastoral charge, it is pertinent to learn and to practice preaching as the ministry to the common life. This we do by recognizing prayerfully our own sure identification with the community of human frailty; by drawing, from above, upon a resource that is versatile and redemptive; by distributing to others the amplitude of God's free grace and undefeatable love. Jesus showed how, as always. He spoke clearly, simply, and seriously. He galvanized the attention of his hearers by means of word pictures,·in humorous asides, and with relentless query. He preached from among the people, to the people, in God's name. So he preached as he taught; he preached as he worshiped; he preached always in ministry to the common life.

Preaching to the Human Condition

Preaching to the common life means first, then, that the preacher speak in God's name, without fear or favor, to the common human condition; that his prophetic ministry be not tempered to some favored group or his cherishing attention be not deflected from some despised category. What this demands, throughout, is that men as a whole be brought to the divine accounting, or, considered from another angle, that the preacher's sermons be constructed and delivered solely to the pleasing of God rather than to the cultivating of public esteem.

Book V of Chrysostom's treatise *On the Priesthood* emphasizes in detail that the preacher who will truly serve all people is one who cannot consider as primary the goal of pleasing any of them. To rank first his desire to please God is the best and only way to serve all men without prejudicial regard for any. Succumbing to the temptation to preach nothing that will offend some is on a tragic par with the calculating plan to say just that which will please certain others. Wholesale praise of the preacher is a pretty sure indication that the divine oracle has been throttled. Frigid silence or warm disapproval by the congregation is of course no proof that the preacher is a prophet, though such popular reaction will be, at some time or other, the prophet's lot.

Cynical or not, Chrysostom decides that, since most people are relatively uncritical, the better the preacher discharges his divine vocation, the less appreciative the multitude will probably be.

It may be poor solace to have Chrysostom reassure us thus: " It follows, of necessity, that he who preaches better than others carries away less applause, and possibly goes home without being praised at all, and he must be prepared to meet such anomalies nobly, and to pardon those who commit them in ignorance, and to weep for those who acquiesce in them on account of envy as wretched and pitiable creatures, and not to consider that his powers have become less on either of these accounts."

That these observations can easily be used for purposes of rationalization, Chrysostom is not wholly unaware. He is, perhaps, on safer ground when he repeats the prime necessity of not regarding as decisive any reaction by the populace — many of whom are so addicted to sermon-tasting and judgment-passing as to be bad for all concerned. The right standard in every instance is the divine imperative registered in the preacher's heart, and the Lord's approbation or rejection vouchsafed to his messenger.

The extent to which John of Antioch followed his own advice is indicated by his sermons delivered on various occasions. One of these series was addressed to people of every class as they cowered together in terror awaiting a common annihilation. Such might easily be the fate of an entire city whose masses had demolished the imperial statues. Chrysostom's pastoral preaching to all groups as one, both before and after these melancholy proceedings, is a tribute to his functioning as a genuine prophet who speaks God's Word without respect to persons. His description of sundry heart-rending experiences that leveled people of all gradations into one common valley of misery is a classic in the history of a preacher's identification with the common life. It is also a landmark in the divinely inspired reassurance to all God's children, in their darkest hour of need.

Well did this same preacher seize the hour after relief from the worst had set in to recapitulate the inner and outer disposition of all classes as they groveled in anticipation of almost certainly impending doom. Nor did he fail in this interval between remembered despair for all, and the not yet fully sensed reprieve for many, to announce the Lord's will that must maintain universally among God's creatures, whether they walked in the light or in the shadow. Thus the sermon begins: As yesterday, " now again I will say, *Blessed be God!* What a day did we see last Wednesday! and what in the present! On that day how heavy was the gloom! How bright the calm of the present! " (6:58).

Then follow pages that make the pulses race and the senses whirl — descriptions of the empty streets, of houses deserted by women and the forums by men; word pictures of wretches, how pitiable, some of them haled into brutal exposure from lately secluded luxury; panoramas of agonized waiting, by others, as relatives and neighbors, on whose testimony the corporate welfare depended, screamed under the lash. " For then, indeed," the preacher reminds his hearers, " wealth, and nobility, and notoriety, and the patronage of friends, and kinship and all worldly things, were found worthless; the sin, and transgression of the law which had taken place, having put all these succours to flight " (6:61).

But now, as Chrysostom preaches, the cries of those under torture have subsided. The shame of proud families has been witnessed in the glaring light of public curiosity. The passions of fear-maddened crowds have been vented to the full; and the deep-lying community of those sharing tragedy has been indelibly stamped on the memory. Such circumstances having receded into never-to-be-forgotten history, the preacher now goes to the consideration of the universal laws that move within, and the timeless forces that drive men without. All the solidarity of mankind evoked in days of concentrated foreboding is, at last, raised aloft in a new context — one called for in the name of

Christian brotherhood and love.

Just as Chrysostom ministered to all his parishioners as to one common family, so he suited his message of the day to the fluctuations of the human spirit. Now he sympathized; again he indicted; always he endeavored to speak as God's man to fellow men.

Gregory the First likewise bore in mind the preacher's obligation to the whole of man. Consequently, he too had regard to the need, now of approving, now of reproving, according to the moods and contradictory qualities of a given man and of the one human condition. " Thus the skilled physician examining a wound which must be lanced, but seeing that the sick man is timid, for some time strokes gently; and then suddenly makes an incision. First he uses the gentle hand of praise, and then the steel of reproof " (15:100).

Quite properly, the preachers in the Great Tradition dealt variously with the same or different people at diverse times, as occasion demanded. But they felt the necessity of ministering to all placed in their care, without respect to persons. Jacques de Vitry, known throughout the Christian world of the mid-thirteenth century, insisted that the pastor of souls must answer impartially the call of the whole flock. Here imitation of the divine involved " the God-like consideration of the poor as of the rich; and not only of the greatest but also of the least, because these minor ones had the major need of consolation." This, of course, did not necessitate an identical treatment of all men's spiritual ills; but it did require a response to the peculiar necessities of one man equal in readiness to that accorded the eccentric demands of another. Thus, to do the different things for different people that their distinctive situations called for was to treat their common humanity in the same Christian way.

The Diversity of the Minister's Service

Greater attention may now be given the proposition that for the preacher to minister thus to the common life was for him to diversify his services as widely as the infinitely ramifiying needs of the one human family demanded.

Alain de Lille in the twelfth century clearly enunciates, and resourcefully amplifies, the old Gregorian principle of preaching to every kind of man the word he especially needs to hear. As the physician of the body suits his treatment to the specific illness, so should the preacher to man's spiritual life.

If the preacher addresses the devotees of wantonness or excess, let him warn its followers to what abominations of God and man it leads. Preaching to the poor, let him commend poverty's advantages and relate such to Christ's own life of renunciation — whose nakedness others in nakedness have followed. Let the rich be warned against wealth's allurements and led to the giving of alms. Soldiers should be admonished to be content with their pay, not plotters of violence; rather ought they be defenders of country and protectors of orphans and widows. When public speakers are exhorted, let them be admonished against espousing unjust causes for gain or in any way commercializing their tongues or prostituting their knowledge. So ought teachers of doctrine to be constrained to the representation of God's will and to the demonstration in fact of what they exhort to in speech. Likewise, the Church's prelates need reminders of their responsibility for godly rule of subordinates, with proper correction and direction. Upon the princes of the earth let there be enjoined the rule of prudence, justice, and mercy, with the utter abomination of avarice.

De Vitry, in his prefaces to sermons for distinctive classes of hearers, indicates with practiced mastery the whole gamut of human experience. The prefaces, and the sermons that fol-

low them, have in mind, for example: prelates and priests of
every kind; monks, nuns, and others in regular orders; barely
literate and erudite men; travelers, crusaders, and professional
soldiers; merchants, farmers, and craftsmen; servants and
slaves of numberless types; as well as virgins, widows, and
those in the married state. Nor are judges, theologians, preachers, ministrants to the sick, those waiting for death to claim
themselves or loved ones, burghers, seafarers, children, and
adolescents forgotten.

It is in one of the several sermons intended for priests that
De Vitry warns his colleagues against preferential treatment,
especially for the wealthy among their parishioners. With the
realism born of long years and careful observation, he reminds
the clergy that the rich are often served, ostensibly, for themselves as human beings; but, actually, in too many instances,
" because money talks." De Vitry attacks those high churchmen who, through their rural deans and other ecclesiastical
subordinates, despoil the poor with specious arguments about
doing them a spiritual service. Such calculating hierarchs sur-
round themselves with lawyers, physicians, and other secular
advisers who will help to fill the institutional coffers; but they
shun the aid of such theologians and truly dedicated religious
assistants as would minister to soul salvation.

The cure of souls is, properly conceived, a vocation from
God and the Spirit to nourish Christ's whole flock; not an invi-
tation to robbers and knaves to plunder the temple. De Vitry
broods over some umbilical parallels between the newborn
infant physically detached from its mother and certain other
blood ties that ought to be cut, but aren't, when advancements
are negotiated. Nepotic promotions are as reprehensible as
they are a commonplace fact.

The doughty preacher has heard of a certain infant pro-
moted by his episcopal uncle to an archdeacon's chair. So

tender was the child's age that he still required the most intimate ministrations of his nurse. De Vitry sternly reminds
his clerical hearers that he who is advanced to ecclesiastical
rulership ought, in the language of Genesis, to say like a
bridegroom to his physical parents, " I know you not." Then
he may cleave to his spouse, that is, the Church. He will there-
upon be free to give his entire love and devotion to the flock
over which he has been set in rulership.

Those who are rectors ought themselves to follow the ways
of rectitude; guardians of the right ought themselves to be
right, declining neither one way nor the other. As Gregory
says, " The art of arts is the rule of souls." De Vitry interlines
this sober wordplay with appropriate references to Bernard,
and others, on the true pastoral function.

With his ever-ready, " I have heard," he tells how some de-
mons are purported to have addressed negligent Sicilian prelates in letters of nethermost affection:

" The princes of the shadows to the princes of the churches,
Greetings! We render thanks to you, because as many as have
been committed to you, so many have been remitted to us."
Audiences in plenty to whom De Vitry preached would have
enjoyed such thrusts considerably more than the one to which
he currently addressed himself. Seven additional sermons to
this same classification of prelates and priests — not to mention a number to preachers and theologians — prove that he
could carry many bucketfuls of water from the same spring
without exhausting its homiletic flow.

But with what change of pace and ministry to pertinent need
Jacques de Vitry proceeded can well be seen in his recently
translated sermon to agriculturists and others. Here the same
bold speaking to the condition before him is directed, now to
employer, now to laborer.

The delight of certain vinedressers and other laborers to

whom he preached one day must have been plainly readable on their faces as De Vitry excoriated penurious employers. Their open glee doubtless congealed in set lines of sheepishness as the preacher continued: " However, there are dishonest laborers who hurry and try to be working hard when the employer is present; but when they are out of sight, they are slow and lazy " (36:195).

The followers of Saint Francis and Saint Dominic carried on a ministry to all men under all manner of specific conditions, as Alain de Lille had called for it and as De Vitry had predicted that they would. Having seen these mendicants at work in Italy and the Holy Land, De Vitry had rejoiced at their apostolic energies released like a ray of light in a world whose sun was fast setting.

Representative of a diversified Dominican appeal are the last portions of Humbert de Romans' volume on *The Education of Preachers*. Here in detailed outline are instructions for preaching scores of sermons for specific occasions and particular groups of hearers. Type sermons are provided for those addressing men as a whole; faithful Christians; people in all grades of literacy; scholars in general; scholars in particular fields; faculties in logic, the liberal arts, and philosophy; students in medicine, common law, civil law, canon law, and theology — to name but a handful. One series would be equivalent to instructing Baptists how to regale Methodists, Presbyterians, et cetera. It is noteworthy also that De Romans was not satisfied with a single sermon type suitable for laymen. He had in mind sermons appropriate for laity at large, laity in the cities, laity in the country, and, thenceforth, those of every conceivable circumstance.

On the Franciscan side, preachers like Berthold in the thirteenth century and Bernardine in the fifteenth were past masters in the art of pilloring distinctive classes of sinners.

They were adept also at speaking to the various problems of the people in their own spiritual language.

Berthold, astounding his hearers with detailed references to the cunning of omnipresent devils, perceives certain reservations on the faces of his listeners. Forthwith he states and answers their unspoken questions: " ' But, Brother Berthold, thou sayest much to us of these devils and of their manifold guiles, and we never see a single devil with our eyes, nor hear we any, nor grasp, nor feel them.' — Lo, now! that is even the worst harm that they do thee; for, didst thou see but once a single devil as he is, then wouldst thou surely never commit one sin again; that itself is one of their snares the worst of all that they have, that they deal so stealthily with us. Now see how dead a silence they keep, albeit there are many thousand of them here in this place! Ye devils, ye hear me well enough preaching here, yet ye would not take all the wealth that is under heaven (I except a man's soul) that only one of you should let himself once be seen; for then all your cunning and your snares would avail you no more. Now see, ye young folk, what a deadly snare that is, that no man may ever see a devil! " (39:211).

But give ear for a moment to Bernardine who is preaching for the day on officeholding and business ethics. "Knowest thou how . . . greedy men . . . act when they are elected to an office? They ask: How much money did such an one get from this office? He got two hundred florins from it. Truly, eh? I shall get three hundred with ease from thence " (55:275). Bernardine's is a classic description of scheming candidates for office, lying in wait for potential voters like a cat settling himself before a tiny mousehole, ready to pounce on the unwary little squeakster as it comes out.

As for his portrayal of unlawful trade practices, attend this exposé of the old counting racket. Here, says the preacher, is how you work your game, counting fast so as to bewilder your victim: " There, and there, and there, and there: one, two, three, five, seven, eight, ten, thirteen, fourteen, sixteen, nineteen, and twenty. And the poor little old woman, who hath not much wit, believeth that it is as thou sayest, and doth receive the money as thou givest it to her; and home she goeth, and doth begin to count it, coin by coin, and findeth herself cheated of three pence, and she returneth to him who gave her the money, and saith: Ay me! I went home with the money you gave me, and I have counted it again; I find that I lack three pence. Such men as this will reply: You will see that you have made a mistake in counting it. Saith she: no, you have given me too little, for the love of God, give it to me. Saith he: Oh! look whether you have not dropped it, hath not your purse perchance a hole in it? And so the poor creature hath the worst of it " (56:285).

Following Bernardine through such sermons on civic responsibility and social obligation, one can hear an undercurrent of injured piety raising the age-old cry, " Why doesn't he stick to the gospel and let politics and economics alone? " To that we can easily imagine Bernardine's courteous reply, " Why don't you try listening to the gospel, to hear what it says about people like you? "

As a comparison of man's wicked ways in country and in town, Brother Berthold, a thirteenth-century Franciscan, and Michel Menot, one of the sixteenth, provide fascinating parallels. After analyzing the defects of town craftsmen with professional thoroughness, Berthold concludes: " But none are so false as the countryfolk among each other, who are so untrue that for envy and hatred they can scarce look upon one another. One will drive another's cattle to his harm and damage, and another will buy his fellow-peasant out of his farm, all from untruth " (38:210–211).

Michel concludes that preachers are expressly directed to large cities: "because more sins are committed there. More wicked men live in large cities than in small villages. Where will you find great and monstrous sins except in cities? Where today are the devourers and torturers of the poor? Certainly there. Abductors and violators of girls, flagrant adulterers, murderers, gormandizers, drunkards, and dissolute men? Certainly in cities. Where now are pomps and vanities? Surely in cities. Where today are the gamblers at cards and dice? Where are gross blasphemy, treachery, envy, slanderers, usurers, cheats, deceivers, and traders on credit? Where today is the dominion of all seven mortal sins? Where is the seat of their power, if not in the great cities? Over the cities Satyricus laments:

> *"What in the future can be gained?*
> *Desires will be the same,*
> *But their achievement lame.*
> *The pinnacle of shame*
> *Is here and now by us attained."*

Furthermore, says Menot, with typically homiletic exaggeration: "The Grace of God is lacking in the great cities. . . . If one man were killed in a country district, everyone for four leagues around would shudder in his whole body at the awfulness of the crime. But in the city, when a good merchant or a court counselor is seen set upon by lewd fellows, or when they seize a modest and pretty girl by her hair and consign her to the brothel, or when a good man is killed in your own quarter; no attention is paid to it" (60:303–304).

In truth, Berthold and Michel, had they been able to participate in a thirteenth- and sixteenth-century symposium, might have got on with relatively minor disagreement. Both would doubtless have argued that whoever made the country and the

city, the devil must be driven out of each; and to that end —
they most certainly would have agreed — God sent preachers
to engage Satan in battle and to announce the Lord's plan of
deliverance for all who would follow the divine will.

PREACHING JUDGMENT AND REDEMPTION

Here again the preachers through the centuries accept the
necessity of preaching to all men both the fearful justice of a
God grievously sinned against and the redemptive love of a
Father revealed in his reconciling Son. Some preachers ex-
celled in drafting the outlines of inescapable judgment; others
rose to the challenge of depicting an ineffably loving redemptiveness. A surprising number balanced their books against the
imminent inspection of the great Auditor who was both sovereign Justice and fatherly Love.

Wulfstan, in the sermon previously alluded to, traced the
decadence of the English to the excessively numerous " ad-
versaries of God, malignant persecutors of the Church, and
cruel tyrants in overgreat number; proud scorners of divine
law and Christian practice "; foolish mockers of God's law;
men " ashamed of good deeds rather than of evil " (21:123)
— inverted hypocrites, as it were. All such he reminded of
ultimate judgment and called upon for a collective as well as
personal revival in the love of God and the adherence to his
laws.

Raoul, with ardor such as Michel later praised, deplored the
threefold darkness of sin, ignorance, and misery. This must
issue, inevitably, in judgment and death. Yet, with a tender-
ness at times approaching that of Francis, he called upon
churchmen and laity to follow the Scriptures as a guiding
light. Through this illumination and the sacrificial revelation
of God's beloved Son, men might endure the present age until
the daystar of divine glory at last dispelled from within them

all darkness of sin, ignorance, and misery — forevermore.

Emphasizing " Christian Fear [as] the Stepping Stone to Christian Love," Peter of Blois lauds those on the way to, and those having arrived at, the Fatherland. These " *press forward to the things that are before* . . . : they not only despise, but are ignorant of fear; and that dread which at first introduced love, being cast out, they, so to speak, cannot help loving ever since the time that they were first inflamed by such affection " (32:173).

With uniquely sensitive insight, Guarric, little-known friend of Bernard, celebrates the humility wherewith the Lord became the servant of men unto the conquering of human pride.

" ' I will not serve the Creator,' says man. ' Then I,' saith the Creator, ' will serve thee, O man. Do thou sit down at the banquet; I will minister to thee, and I will wash thy feet. Do thou rest; I will bear thy sicknesses — I will carry thine infirmities. . . . If thou art an hungered or athirst, and hast nothing at hand . . . behold, I myself am ready to be sacrificed, that thou mayest eat My Flesh and drink My Blood. And fear not that, from the death of thy servant, thou wilt suffer the loss of his service: after thou hast fed upon Me, I shall remain whole and alive, and I will serve thee as I did before.' "

To this self-immolating love must man finally succumb and cry out: " So it is — so it is that Wisdom conquers Malice. So Thou hast heaped coals of fire upon the head of obstinate man, that by them he might be inflamed to penitence. Thou hast conquered, therefore, O Lord, Thou hast conquered the rebel! Lo! I yield myself to Thy fetters, and I put my neck under Thy yoke " (31:169, 171).

THE ACTIVE AND THE CONTEMPLATED LIFE

In the pre-Reformation period, as since, true preachers to the common life sought to emphasize a proper balance between the demands of the active and the contemplative. Christian preaching took into consideration the social scene, as well as the inward experience of individual men and women. The kind and degree of transformation sought and achieved have their debatable aspects. That representative ministers of the gospel throughout the early and medieval periods tried to make a place for both the worshipful love of God and the active love of neighbor seems beyond dispute.

Gregory, in his *Moralia*, declares that " he is no perfect preacher, who either, from devotion to contemplation, neglects works that ought to be done, or, from urgency in business, puts aside the duties of contemplation. . . . It is hence that the Redeemer of mankind in the day time exhibits His miracles in cities, and spends the night in devotion to prayer upon the mountain, namely, that He may teach all perfect preachers, that they should neither entirely leave the active life, from love of the speculative, nor wholly slight the joys of contemplation in excess of working, but in quiet imbibe by contemplation, what in employment they may pour back to their neighbours by word of mouth. For by contemplation they rise unto the love of God, but by preaching they return back to the service of their neighbour."

So, too, Francis of Assisi demonstrated, in this connection, the conclusion that various sources attribute to him. He had called upon his friends to help him to discover, according to the divine will, whether he " should attend to preaching or only to prayer." He heard gladly their common conviction: " Christ has answered and revealed that it is His will for you to go out into the world and preach; for He has not chosen you for yourself alone, but also for the salvation of others."

John Tauler, like Saint Francis, gives the lie, with other mystics, to the charge of unadulterated individualism leveled at cultivators of the inner life. Tauler insists that inner love for God and outer regard for fellows should go together. " But it sometimes happens that men can think deeply of our Lord in their interior soul, but yet are spiritually superficial — like a wide stretch of water of scarcely a finger's depth. Now, the reason is that they are deficient in real humility, and they lack a universal love for their fellowmen " (47:243). With laudable balance Tauler advises against sheer busyness and social activism, for those lacking inner resources of prayer and contemplation; just as he summons outward, and society-ward, those given too exclusively to spiritual withdrawal. One of the acid tests as to whether or not the soul hears the inward, eternal Word is that which measures devotion in terms of consideration for all men: " Again, thy universal spiritual exercise should be sincere love of all mankind, not only the members of thy own community, but all priests and monks and nuns and sisters, and all humanity besides, of whatever state or condition; and this love should be active " (48:248).

The works of Thomas Aquinas are generally adduced as favoring contemplative piety — which they do. Nonetheless, they have their surprising quota of concern for the active investment of inward resources, to be released in service to one's fellows.

All-important, in this area, is the main line of precedence. One worships the divine first, then serves the human. Humanity is not its own end; nor is the Kingdom of God its product. The eternal community given from above elicits the temporal society answering from below. Beginnings do not determine ends, so much as ends draw out beginnings. Christ who goes before lures unto himself those who are his. The Church becomes the servant of the eternal Kingdom in the temporal world.

Quite appropriately, a sermon of Augustinian lineage combines the building of a physical church and the construction of the Church that is heavenly. With Paul, the preacher exclaims: "For Christ, our Foundation, is set above, that we may be built upward (cf. Col. 2:7). For a building of earthly materials, whose heavy mass can fall only downwards, the foundation is placed underneath. On the contrary for us, the foundation stone is set above, that He may draw us upward by the force of His love " (14:93).

With pregnant phrase, Cusa declares:

" But just as the art of living well in this world is variously revealed by various insights, and the clearer these are, the more perfect it is, so also religion, which looks to the future life and orders the present for the sake of the future, has been variously revealed by prophets foreseeing the future from a distance. And because no one sees the future life except in imagination, therefore only he, who came into our human nature from God and that heavenly life which is future for us, could perfectly reveal religion or the way to it. This is our Jesus, who came from Heaven that we might have life and live more abundantly through him than through nature, who [also] ' began to do and to teach ' how this might be accomplished. . . . He who was also the Way of nature was himself, therefore, the Way to the attainment of grace " (58:293–294).

Thus the preachers in the Great Tradition contended in theory for that which, like ourselves, they found difficult of practical application. Throughout the Christian gospel they sensed corporate experience and individual metamorphosis to be, as it were, in equilibrium. However inadequately applied, the appeal to fashion the past and present over the forms of the future had certain advantages. It was emancipated from the tyranny of things as they are and have been. It was dedicated to the transformation of this world, from above and beyond, rather than accommodated to the natural hegemony of things, from behind and beneath.

POPULAR PREACHING AND SERMON ILLUSTRATION

If there be those who doubt that such a message could ever have been preached to the common, human condition, let them remember one thing: Earlier times were not devoid of richly inventive means for giving profound truths a popular appeal. Surely much, if not most, preaching to the faithful was done in the vernacular language and with the universal vocabulary of homespun suggestion. Rhyming sermonettes on themes such as animal bondage to earth and human aspiration toward heaven are evidence, in their very popularity, of a common man's theology. But the masters of its exposition were uncommonly perceptive and versatile.

By far the most fruitful field of exploitation in the whole area of popular preaching in the thirteenth century, and after, was the extended use of *exempla,* that is, examples, or sermon illustrations. An analysis of the prevailing types of *exempla* as they came to be utilized in the late patristic and medieval ages is especially valuable at this time. There are twelve basic types of such examples which the preacher drew upon most heavily. The first of these is primarily Biblical and finds its chief emphases in the historical books of the Old and New Testaments, together with legendary recitals from the Jewish-Christian tradition. A second involves writings of the Fathers and ecclesiastical authors, drawing particularly upon the *Lives of the Fathers* and other associated sayings of well-known people in religious vocations. The third classification is mainly hagiographical. Here the *Acts of the Saints* is the major point of derivation. The variations are endless. Local as well as universal illustrations from the lives of the saints are added to the edifying miracles of the Virgin and to the accounts developed in connection with eucharistic celebrations. Yet another category is mainly concerned with the retailing of visions and apparitions. This, of course, had its ready users throughout the whole Christian Era. A fifth set of materials is largely secular in its foundation and gathers edifying stories with regard to philosophers, historians, and moralists, whether they be Greek, Roman, Persian, or any other group of men.

A sixth classification deals chiefly with historic events. The provenance may be in terms of world history or local scene. War episodes, stories coming out of heresies and the combating of them, and the doings of famous men, all find a place here. Another type is more strictly legendary, in the sense that it is drawn from chronicles, epic poems, and the fabulous in history, whether near or remote in origin. Closely related are an eighth and a ninth set of classifications involving the celebrated conte and the fable. The first is more concerned with animals, parables, and the like. The fable is not too far removed from it. Together these easily make for interesting little dramas, in which animals and men have a fascinating interchange of functions and an amusing substitution of characteristics. De Vitry knows how to use these very well. Bozon is a master of the conte. The so-called *moralité* group employs a large amount of allegory, and is easily related and sometimes confused with another classification known as that of the *prodigé*. Here prodigious happenings, occurring in demonstration of the secrets of nature, require a more than natural explanation. Lastly, there is the *exemplum* of a highly personal nature which gives the preacher using it a full opportunity to tell about his own travels and his contacts with people under every conceivable social condition. The way in which he could bring in his own deep religious experiences and commend them to his always impressionable audience need not be labored at this point.

MASTERS OF VERNACULAR PREACHING

With Jacques de Vitry, in mid-thirteenth century, we encounter a master in the art of popular sermon illustration. The *common life*, to him, meant the life of all people — rich and poor, humble and great, churchman and soldier, monk and slave, pilgrim and scholar, merchant and farmer, virgin and married woman, peasant and king. It was to these, with all their kaleidoscopic appeal, that De Vitry preached. It was these, also, that he scolded with impunity, cajoled upon occasion, and prayerfully implored to lead a better life, together with himself. It is increasingly apparent that De Vitry followed no absolute formula in approaching his preaching problem. Sometimes he used a particular formula; sometimes he did not. Almost always he used illustrations, usually with great effectiveness.

In one of his sermons to working people De Vitry gives a catena of examples that show how tragically people fail in their Sabbath observation. He has not only heard tales of them, but he has observed situations in which people have no idea of what day the Sabbath is; they depend entirely upon the silence of the woodsman's ax or the absence of the farmer's cart from the fields to know that it must be the Lord's Day. Apropos of the cavalier attitude of many people who neglect feast days or are completely ignorant of their proper times, De Vitry tells how, in a certain town, an old rustic by the name of Gocelinus kept the people's calendar of church days for them. Having from long habit learned the religious festivals, he put on his red shoes on the days appropriate to local observance. His neighbors, seeing this, would say, " Today we must rest from work and go to church for Gocelinus has on his red shoes " (cf. 36:197).

Many of these instances are not, technically speaking, *ex-*

empla at all. They are simply a running commentary drawn, with surprising versatility, from everyday experience as the common laborers knew it. In the sermon to vinedressers De Vitry boasts his usual fund of crisp, short stories. There is the rich man who saved a pie so long that, when it was cut for his guests, the mice ran out. The preacher has even heard of stingy folks who make a short coat out of a cloak, a jacket from the coat, slippers from the jacket, and, finally, half shoes from the slippers — all this so that the poor may be defrauded of their dues. Such people " prefer to have the mice, rather than the poor, keep themselves warm in the clothes which they allow to grow mouldy on clothes racks. But the handsomest clothes rack for a rich man is the body of a poor man where garments are kept safe and not eaten by moths nor stolen by thieves " (36:193).

FRIAR BOOKS OF SERMONS AND ILLUSTRATIONS

The real heirs of De Vitry's vogue were, of course, the Dominicans and Franciscans. Not only did they write preaching manuals in which they taught the use of *exempla;* they also gave homiletic demonstration of their theories. Étienne de Bourbon, of the thirteenth century, served the Dominican Order in a variety of positions, including that of inquisitor. One discerns in him an apparently able expositor; here also is an individual who knows how to develop structural systems of thought out of both simple and profound sources. He writes his chief work on *The Diversity of Preaching Materials.* It is not necessary to enumerate all the areas from which he draws his support. It is much more important to remember that he has found certain bold divisions that lend themselves quite well to his purpose. In organizing his data, for instance, about the seven gifts of the Holy Spirit, he has ample opportunity to enumerate infinite subheadings which fall under the larger

classifications of fear, piety, knowledge, and might. His outline alone is a tribute to the resourcefulness of his mind and
the lasting qualities of his energy. Like De Vitry and others
before him, he has gathered together materials that are appropriate for all sorts of individuals in all types of social gatherings. But he, like his predecessors, is genuinely concerned to
provide some sermonic data that will be helpful in the formation of the religious life for simple folk. This means almost
unnumbered *exempla*. And he believes that such illustrations
may be used with wholesome effect, not only in turning men's
eyes toward the eternal world, but in helping them to live good
lives in everyday association with their fellow men.

John Bromyard's massive collection of materials on every
conceivable subject that might affect the preaching art is one
of the most remarkable of the whole Middle Ages. As a fourteenth-century Dominican, and a theological professor at Cambridge, he evidenced the same quality of interest in the careful collection and organization of data that was observable
among both the Franciscans and the Friar-Preachers. Naturally, he gave a large place to *exempla*. He showed, with pa-
tient attention to a host of fundamental Christian doctrines,
how one might take a profound subject and illustrate it quite
simply with a virtually inexhaustible set of illustrations. His
table of contents alone suggests the wealth of matters contained in his book. With, perhaps, the most superbly organized
grasp of all the medieval manuals, John's *Summa* provides a
solidly patristic and Biblical background for reflections upon
melancholy, eternal bliss, war, labor, trade, prayer, the ministry, simony, society, the Holy Spirit, and many more. Sup-
pose, by way of experiment, the reader turns to the treatment
of " Preachers " and " Preaching "; his initial distaste at the
wooden organization and treatment of items soon gives way to
admiring regard for the mass of pertinent materials so care-

fully selected and the complementary subjects so logically re-lated to them.

If the Dominicans were more systematic, as compilers of ex-amples within handbooks, the Franciscans were more oppor-tunistic, as exploiters of sermonic storytelling. The Sienese prophet Bernardine talked about a wide variety of subjects as he spoke to the people in university towns, in the near-rural areas, and on the fringes of the great urban centers of com-merce. He illustrated the characteristics of human life wherever he found them, with any and all instruments of pulpit effec-tiveness available.

Who of us would be prepared for the story of how an ape and a bear demonstrated the principle of justice?

" Lo! I wish to tell you an example which happened in the court of the king of France, or of the king of Spain. He had an ape and a bear, and he kept them for his disport. It happened that the ape having young, the bear killed one little ape and devoured it. The ape seeing what had been done, it seemed as if she were crying out for justice, for she betook herself to well nigh all those of the household; she turned now to one side, and now to the other, about each one of those whom she saw. And seeing that she was not understood, one day she broke her chain and went to that place wherein was the bear; for it seemed as if she said: since that no one doth execute justice in respect of the crime of this bear, I myself will exe-cute it. In that place where was the bear there was much hay. This ape took some of the hay and collected it together around and about the bear; in sum, she put fire to it and burned the bear, and in this manner herself executed justice. — Seest thou that the beasts endeavour in every way that justice be exe-cuted, and render that which is merited according to the deed which the other hath performed. — And by this thou dost see that nature dictates it to thee " (55:272–273).

Which of us would dare launch forth before the women of his audience upon an illustration of domestic economy such as this?

" Hist! I would explain so that I may be understood by these women. Women, if you have a spindle, not too large, or a paternoster, one of those which are very large, put your middle finger upon the spindle and your next finger to this also upon the paternoster, and you shall see that they will seem each one of them two. Now make trial of it, quickly, that I may see you do so for a little " (55:273). Bernardine's application then follows.

Obviously, this preacher not only retails stories of wolves thwarted of their prey, and of crows taking liberty with scarecrows; he also makes his examples as he goes, from among his hearers. For the purpose of illustrating the burdens of office, he needs an example of physical burden-bearing and how one becomes stooped in his walk. He calls out to his congregation: " Is there no porter here? Oh, porters! when you have a sack of wheat on your back, you know in truth that you walk thus a little stooped, and the greater the weight the more dost thou stoop forward " (55:277).

Preaching often in the open square, with every species of competing interest all about, Bernardine has to catch, hold, and recover attention. To a noisy vender he calls out in the course of his sermon — " Oh, you there at the fountain, who are selling your wares, go and do so elsewhere! Do you not hear me, O you there at the fountain? Home again! " (55:272). But Bernardine really holds his own, quite well.

Actually there is little point in laboring the matter. We are proud today, and justly so, of talents such as Walt Disney's. These reflect for us in face-saving animal mirrors the foibles and accomplishments of lordly man. But at least three preachers in the Great Tradition, mentioned in this chapter, could outdo Disney and his indentured Hollywood servants. These preachers were without the benefit of movie-making legerdemain. Nevertheless, they captured on the retina of the spiritual eye the universal experience of average man. Projecting what they saw, as on a magic screen, they set moving again, with the aid of living words, the whole vast panorama of the common life.

Chapter Four

PREACHING THE WORD
AND THE MINISTRY OF WORSHIP

PREACHING the Word and the ministry of worship must proceed together. They cannot long be separated if man is to live, spiritually. If the gospel word of Christ is preached, it is to the end that God may be worshiped; if the Lord be worshiped, his will for man must forthwith be preached to the world in Christ's name. Jesus read, and gave exposition to, the sacred writings in the synagogue, in the house of prayer and instruction. In synagogue, in Temple, and outside, he preached God's Word, so that his people might be reconciled to the Most High in worship. Like Jeremiah, he went to the Temple to worship with his people; he stayed, like Jeremiah, to declare the judgment of God upon the perversion of that worship.

The apostles' action in Acts 6:1–4 was not unchristian: the ministry of " Word and worship " must come first if there is ever to be a ministry to widows and orphans. The Early Church habitually couples proclamation of the gospel message and corporate prayer of the faithful. The *Apologies* of Justin and Tertullian show this same predominance of worship — giving rise to fraternal considerations of the most specific kind. The greatest sermons of all the ages grow out of worship — and call men to it. The most persistent contention, if not the most con-sistent adornment, of medieval times is that the Word and the service of worship shall be knit into a constant whole. The message of our Reforming progenitors is that the Word must be properly proclaimed and heard, and the Sacraments properly administered and participated in, if the true Church is to exist.

The ministry of preaching has its distinctive functions and responsibilities; so also has the ministry of worship. Indiscriminate confusion of the two brings embarrassment and tragedy. To bow before the Lord, to take the Lord's body and blood, does not make any less necessary the clear exposition of the gospel. This the pre-Reformation Church too often forgot. To preach and teach the full import of the gospel does not mean that the acts of private and public worship can be bypassed or curtailed. The Reformers realized this, but many of their followers have forgotten. Thus all too many Christians, however earnest, have scissored and pasted the gospel to make it fit into an ingeniously derived and mysteriously impressive liturgy. Others, no less honest and perverse, have stolen from the altar to support the pulpit.

But the Christian road to God has always been a united pilgrimage of " Word and worship." This the Early Church felt in a great blaze of intercommunion. This was the passionate witness to the living Christ and the reverent obeisance to the divine purpose that made Christianity real — whenever it was real — in the first fifteen hundred years of its history. This, the Luthers, the Calvins, the Wesleys rediscovered and reapplied. This, today, we often subserve with acquiescent minds and embroider with patronizing unconcern. But preaching, properly conceived, calls for disciplined thought and specific demands. And worship, rightly entered into, puts us on our knees, where our own voices are muffled long enough to let our hearts and heads fill with an eternal message.

The Use of the Bible in Preaching

One must acknowledge forthwith the unquestioned centrality of the Bible in Origen, Chrysostom, and Augustine. There is a continuation of Biblical references and quotations, at least, in the period of homiletic decadence from the sixth to the twelfth century. Here one observes a large degree of dependence on the earlier patristics for Biblical usage as in practically all else. The frequently encountered appreciation for medieval Biblical knowledge among preachers is both true in a high degree and false in many of its commonly accepted implications. The sermons of the whole period are the best testimony, at one and the same time, to continuing Biblical usage of a sort, and to the appeal for something more than the all-too-perfunctory, stylized method of appropriating the Scriptures, then generally in vogue.

We cannot ignore the obvious unfairness of many modern strictures that would make medieval preaching devoid of any genuinely Scriptural quality. Nor can we pass by, any more readily, the distorted character of those generalizations that make Bernard of Clairvaux's Bible mastery, or Gerson's Scriptural concern, in any sense typical. Highly questionable matter and method were often employed by those who did use the Bible extensively and intensively.

" The very real virtues and marked limitations of medieval Bible usage among preachers is put into perspective by researches in manuscripts and printed works like those of [Owst,] Deanesly, and Smalley " (NUS, p. 10). Extensive Biblical quotations and references may at times indicate a generous use of concordances rather than any great mastery of the Book. Nonetheless, the detailed admonitions and the personal practices of many a devoted medieval preacher are not to be discounted arbitrarily. Grosseteste, Bonaventura, Eckhart, Tauler, Wyclif,

Gerson, and Savonarola made consistently effective use of the Scriptures in their sermons. Still, the very burden of much of their preaching was the declared poverty of Biblical understanding within their own profession. Doubtless, a part of the caustic disparagement of medieval Bible preaching by modern critics is due to relative ignorance of the ends sought and the methods employed.

Deanesly reminds us that, for England at least, the early medieval homily, founded on a text of the Sunday Gospel or Epistle, had some continuance throughout the Middle Ages. Her contention is equally well supported, however, that this was limited in value as a teaching institution by the comparative infrequency of sermons and the tendency to discard the Sunday Gospel as a subject in later times. It is hard to meet her further objection that the priests' accountability for teaching the faith, rather than expounding the Bible, was what bishops and synods insisted upon, from the early Middle Ages to the Reformation.

Furthermore, preaching in the Middle Ages was peculiarly the word of the Church, not the independent exposition of the Scriptural preacher, per se. As councils and popes took pains to declare, the preacher's word was the word of God as the institutional Church authorized it.

This may seem to us as it often did to Wyclif, and others like him, all too little dominated by the power of the naked gospel. But to Francis, Bernard, and others, this was the only way the Word could truly come — in terms of the Church to which, in the person of Peter, Christ had given the keys to the Kingdom of Heaven. Proclaiming the terms of Kingdom entrance, as well as the operation of the sacramental powers giving entrance to the eternal realm, was the province of the Church's clergy.

It was precisely because Christ was thought to have given

Peter and his successors the right to bind and loose that preachers must conform to the pattern of his divinely empowered institution. This was likewise the reason that the sermon held its chief obligation to be the interpretation of the mysteries celebrated in the liturgy.

Gradually emerging in the sharpness of their definition and in the description of their efficacy, the Sacraments, administered by a properly validated priesthood and hierarchy, become the means whereby man, with all his natural limitations, may be reconciled to God. Sinful humanity thus finds its way into the supernatural fellowship of all those enjoying the beatific vision. For medieval man, following the catholicizing trends advanced by Augustine, the ultimate fellowship with God in the company of saints and angels becomes the end product toward which all human society moves. The eucharistic bread nourishes the pilgrim on the way to his eternal homeland. In the high Middle Ages these well-defined Sacraments are conceived of, and proclaimed, as the Lord's indispensable way to an endless and thoroughly social beatitude.

To consult the missal is to be reminded that Scriptural materials implanted in the worship of the Christian year constitute a rich thesaurus of things Biblical. Further recognition should be instantaneous that in the awesome services made efficacious in the Church's — not the people's — language, the full appropriation of these treasures must be largely dependent on the priestly interpreter, his learning, and his edificatory powers. Here the visual aids of sculpture, window imagery, and the whole symbolism of Christian art do their incomparable work. They must succeed through their articulation with architectural purpose and iconographic ends in facilitating the spiritual tryst of the worshiper with his Lord, in the company of Biblical personalities and beloved saints. If the priest makes his admonition such as to reveal with simplicity the deep re-

sources of the gospel promises, as they are mirrored in stone
or glass, while he joins his parishioners' everyday experiences
to the age-old faith intoned in the chants and proclaimed in the
lessons of the Mass, then the Bible, however adapted and selected, may still be a factor indeed. But if, for whatever reason,
he fails, the gospel that the people need may be almost as non-
existent or distorted as Wyclif declares it to be.

To be sure, the greater number of vigorous Bible preachers
in the Middle Ages preached, however short or long, in the
context of the liturgical services being celebrated for a given
day. It was thus that Francis, having heard and understood, to
a degree, the intent of gospel renunciation, heard further the
priest's exposition, presumably both in the sermon and afterward; and so he came to espouse Lady Poverty.

Preaching the gospel, however underemphasized as such,
was still implied, in the Middle Ages, to the extent that interpretation of Christ's Sacraments involved some proclamation
of his Word. History testifies that the extent of such proclamation varied from virtually nothing to abundantly much. True,
little is said regarding the preaching function in such a handbook as Myrc's *Instructions for Parish Priests*. But the burden
of its emphasis is upon the doctrinal, liturgical, and moral
qualities that preaching strives to inculcate. With Wyclif the
case is quite different.

PREACHING IN RELATION TO WORSHIP

Before treating in detail Wyclif's major contributions, however, it will be advisable to observe, somewhat more fully,
representative preaching of the Word in relation to worship.

Origen, with all his penchant for the spiritualized interpretation of the Word, held that " there is not one jot or one tittle
written in Scripture which, for those who know how to use the
power of the Scriptures, does not effect its proper work.

144 54

" It is like the case of herbs; each has its power, whether for
health of the body or for some other purpose. But it is not for
every one to understand the purpose for which each herb is
useful." As with the expert in herbs, " the saintly man is a sort
of spiritual herbalist, culling from the sacred Scriptures each
jot, each chance letter, and discovering the force of the letter
and the purpose for which it is of use, and that nothing written
is devoid of meaning " (2:47). For this cause, Christ and his
Church enlighten the mind and make the soul ready for the reception of spiritual truth. Putting the Kingdom first will not
permit the true Christian to assign but " one hour or two out
of the whole day to God, just coming to the church for prayer,
giving a passing attention to the word of God, but devoting his
main interest to the concerns of the world and of his appetite."

Chrysostom, likewise, in the eleventh homily on Saint John,
emphasized the indispensable preparation of every Christian for
worship and preaching, through reading the Scriptures before
the service. So well, in fact, did he stress the people's gospel-
receptivity that Faber, in the preface to his French translation
of the New Testament, in 1523, cited Chrysostom's authorita-
tive Scriptural injunction.

In the third book of Chrysostom's work *On the Priesthood*,
John had, in addition, held up to somber gaze the terrifying
responsibility of the priest through whose functions, properly
discharged, men escaped hell and entered the Kingdom of
Heaven. The priest who would celebrate the saving rites of
the Church is also the one who must administer the divine
healing through the " powerful application of the Word."
" Wherefore," says Chrysostom, " it should be our ambition
that the Word of Christ dwell in us richly." For laity, as for
the priesthood, Word and worship belong together.

The manner in which a devoted medieval preacher might develop a Scriptural theme and foster thereby the sense of re-

sponsible worship on the part of the faithful is exemplified by Hrabanus Maurus in the ninth century. In a sermon for Sundays, Maurus comments on the Biblical injunction to keep the Sabbath holy: "Let us see therefore that our rest be not in vain; but from the evening of the Saturday to the evening of the Sunday, have nothing to do with any country work, or any other business, and give yourself up to God's worship only. Thus shall we rightly sanctify the Sabbath of the Lord. . . . Let every one therefore who can, come to vespers and to nocturns, and there pray in the congregation of the Church, confessing his sins to God. And he who cannot do so much, at least let him pray in his own house, and not neglect to pay his vows to God, and to render the service due to Him. And, on the day itself, let no one fail to attend the holy celebration of Mass, nor remain idle at home, when others are going to church; let no man occupy himself about hunting, and engage in the devil's work; nor roam about the fields and woods, shouting and laughing, instead of raising from his heart sighs and prayers to God." Some, Maurus knows, " who come to church, neither enter, nor pray, nor wait with silence for the celebration of Mass; but when the lessons are being read within, they are either transacting law business, or indulging in calumny without, or giving themselves up to dice or to useless games." " Do not," the preacher says, " give your attention, outside, to vain talk; but within to psalms and prayers." Quietness should prevail. "For there are many, and principally women, who so chatter in church, who so keep on talking, that they neither hear the lessons themselves, nor allow others to hear them " (18:112–113).

Raoul Ardent has left us a sermon, based on II Peter 1:12–15, in which he capitalizes this apostle's gospel teaching in a distinctive plea for Scriptural life. The appeal for true pastors to proclaim the Word and for the genuinely faithful to hearken to the Holy Word is an integral part of a regular worship service. Unfortunately, charges the preacher, contemporary "pastors are neither themselves mindful of the Scriptures, nor do they make others mindful. They strive for worldly wealth. In aim and deed, they show themselves to be not shepherds but hirelings. . . . Are there not today prelates who are in the Church, not in order to benefit souls, but in order that they themselves may be exalted, honored, and entertained? They do not ask in which church they can aid more souls, but in which church they can collect more money, find more opportunity for profitable selling" (24:130). No wonder the people charge the priest with preaching "to extract the cash." This, of course, does not justify recreant sheep any more than it absolves careless shepherds. Both need to do penance: the pastors should proclaim the Word; the laity should heed its voice.

Saint Peter had asserted in substance: Not fables, but truth and wisdom we make known to you. "By these words," says Raoul, "he condemns those who ignore the Gospels and read poetic fables, bucolic songs, and comedies. For boys, this may have the excuse of necessity; but for others, it is a voluntary offense" (24:131). The preacher, himself a man of culture and scholarship, seems to be admitting certain prerogatives of the classical arts; but they have no rights comparable to those of the gospel.

Raoul insists that Scriptural neglect is an alarming sign of the times. Peter condemns, together with clergy who will not preach the Bible, "those who are unwilling to pay attention to the reading of the Scriptures. There are many such . . . [in Raoul's day] even among officials of Holy Church, who scorn the Scriptures and pursue hawking, hunting, dice, sports, and idle amusements; who even despise the Holy Scriptures and pursue secular law, law-suits, and vain inventions. With these words the ordinary people also are blamed, because they prefer to hear popular songs, banjos, and idle shows rather than the Holy Scripture." How do pastors and people hope to emerge from the threefold darkness of sin, ignorance, and misery without the sacred Word? "The Holy Scripture is truly a light for us in this world" (24:134).

Such a sermon, preached within the worship service — and on a festival day at that — is, like the one of Maurus, an enlightening example of Word and worship conjoined in the same ministry.

Bernardine of Siena, in a colloquial fifteenth-century sermon, gives preaching a seeming precedence over the Mass itself. The Church, he tells his hearers, demands that there be preaching every Sunday — "much or little, but some preaching." Uneasy listeners sense that this preacher will never settle for any such minimal requirements. Now, they think, is the time for those already having heard a Sunday sermon to escape. But the preacher is wide-awake. With a deft pat of his casuistical paw he pins down these homiletic mice about to scurry for freedom. Then he continues: The Church "hath ordered thee to go to hear Mass, and if of these two duties thou canst perform but one, that is either hear Mass or hear the preaching, thou shouldst rather lose Mass and hear the preaching; since the reason for this doth appear plainly, thou dost not so endanger thy soul by not hearing Mass as by not listening to the preaching" (54:270).

His listeners are caught off guard this time for a certainty. This will take some explaining. And the preacher readily obliges with some neat yo-yo logic. He gives a little — a little time for his major premise to pique their curiosity. He takes a little — a little advantage of their bewilderment over his minor premise. Then he puts the whole situation in his pocket — safely stowed away are the popular interest and the chance to drive home his conclusions without interruption.

Yes! hearing the preaching may be more important than hearing the Mass, for if they hear the preaching they will surely learn how imperative it is for them to hear the Mass. Perhaps some of his more intelligent hearers have an intuitive feeling that this is where they came in. But the preacher now has the revolving door moving fast, and they swing around with it.

"For tell me," he triumphantly concludes, "should you believe in the Blessed Sacrament of the Altar if this had not been preached in holy sermons? Thou hast learned to believe in the Mass only from preaching. More than this, how ever shouldst thou have known what sin is, if not from preaching?" And, he reminds them further, knowledge of hell as of every good, and of heaven's glories themselves, come "to thee through the words heard by thine ears, and it is in thiswise that thou comest by knowledge to faith, and that which thou knowest and which thou hast hath come all through the word of God. And this is a sovereign rule, that which we have of the faith of Jesus Christ hath come merely through preaching. And this faith will never perish while it shall be preached" (54:270–271). With whatever argumentative license employed, the preacher has so lodged the inseparability of Word and worship in the popular consciousness as to have an indefinite option on the people's continuing suggestibility.

On closer investigation, these words, which sound so much like Wyclif's, do not end as his do with a near replacement, by the preaching of "Goddis Lawe," of all other credos, paternosters, aves, and even institutional sacraments, themselves. This gospel of Bernardine's is neither so nude nor so bold as Wyclif's "naked text." But it is stripped for action, and it is persistent in its solicitation.

One cannot but remember Humbert de Romans' sentiment that without such preaching the fullness of celestial glory cannot be consummated. With it alone the overflow of infernal designs can be effectively checked. When preaching ceases, the world becomes sterile and undergoes thralldom to demonic forces. No longer does the human heart swell with hopes of a heavenly fatherland. Where preaching is in abeyance, Christian nations fall off and the Church itself declines. Indispensable indeed is the office of preaching when its absence throws the whole world into shadow, brings about evil and pestilence, depopulates cities, and estops the waters of civilization at their very source.

Ironical, is it not, that two of the orders so despised by Wyclif — the Dominicans, represented by Humbert de Romans before him, and the Franciscans, typified by Bernardine of Siena after him — should come closest to his own sentiment?

WYCLIF'S BIBLE PREACHING

But what exactly did Wyclif think of Scriptural preaching in relation to the Church's worship? For what he preached, he too articulated with the liturgical calendar. A précis of his views is now in order. In his Latin works, as in the English writings attributed to him, John Wyclif places a high estimate upon the function of preaching. "The first and greatest work of the priest is the promulgation of religious truth." A series of like declarations, drawn variously from his prolific writings, assert that the telling of the gospel story is the most important duty of the pastor. Next to living a just life, nothing that he can do is more important than this. It actually surpasses the place given to the administration of the Sacraments. Wyclif quotes Robert Grosseteste, bishop of Lincoln, as saying that of all the works of Christian charity " none is nobler, better, and more to be desired than preaching." A whole chapter of Wyclif's *On the Pastoral Office* (II, 2) is given to this treatment. Christ himself would not have commissioned his apostles to preach the gospel unto all mankind had he not thought the sermon most important of those works required at the hands of an apostle or curate. Wyclif recalls Saint Augustine's reminder that the conversion of heathenism in so short a time, by such simple men as the apostles, was a greater miracle than any other that Christ performed following his incarnation. In a real sense, it is Christ himself who speaks in the preacher. The preacher is but the Lord's medium and has no claim to merit for that which Christ speaks through him.

An emphasis that is found throughout Wyclif's Latin and English sermons — and indeed the whole corpus of his writings — is that which makes preaching the means whereby the Church draws the temporal society into the fold of the heavenly community. " By means of preaching, Christ creates for Himself [here on earth] heirs of the heavenly kingdom." Again Wyclif insists that even the simplest theologian can scarcely fail to place the sermon far above every other earthly work; it is the most precious function of the Church, even excelling prayer and the Sacraments. The very life and word of God the Trinity appear in the sermon. Hence, any failure on the part of priest or people to deliver or to hear it results in tragedy. In a section that certainly sounds less than completely Catholic, Wyclif declares that it would be far better " if bishops would preach and teach the catholic faith, instead of dispensing such things as sacraments, or consecrating churches."

Wyclif's thought is well summarized in Dr. J. Loserth's recapitulation of Latin Sermon 57 (Part II) : " Christ has said: Go out and proclaim that the kingdom of heaven is at hand. One must preach of the kingdom of heaven, of the kingdom of Christ, of the Lord's Advent, of the Church militant, the Church triumphant, and of the universal or catholic Church, of the old and the new law, but above all of Christ and His incarnation, and of the preparation of man for eternal blessedness. As the time is already at hand in which Christ prepares man for obtaining this blessedness, the preacher must exhort his hearers 'to set to work' in order to obtain it. This it is which must be preached to the people, not tragedies or comedies or fictions or apocryphal sentences, as is the habit of preachers in these days."

It is just for this reason that Wyclif insists on having the Scriptures preached to the people in their mother tongue. If they are to appreciate the conditions of salvation upon which their entry to the eternal commonwealth depends, they must hear the Lord's own word in a fashion that they can understand. Nor does Wyclif's doctrine of election compromise in the least his conviction that those who are to be saved are to be called to their predestined heritage by the preached Word.

In an English sermon purportedly his, Wyclif stresses the imminent judgment:

"Sad belief [earnest faith] of this third Advent should stir men from sin and draw them to virtues. For if they should tomorrow answer to a judge, and win great rents or else lose them, they would full busily shape for their answer, and much more if they should win or lose their life. Lord! since we be certain of the day of doom that it shall come to us, and we wit not how soon, and there we shall have judgment of heavenly life, or else of deep of hell that evermore shall last, how busy should we be to make us ready for this! Certes, default of belief is cause of our sloth, and thus should we fasten in us articles of the truth, for they will be loose in us as nails in a tree, and therefore it is needful to knock and make them fast."

It is a striking commentary on his whole series of English works, which the Latin series of sermons likewise sustains, that Wyclif specifically admonishes the clergy to use this time for the spreading of the vernacular gospel. Thus souls may be won for the heavenly Kingdom. In the discharge of this responsibility, bishops and other high ecclesiasts cannot rid themselves of their own proper obligation. Substitutes are not an adequate answer to the bishop's own individual duties. Every priest, the bishop included, should give immediate and unqualified attention to the task, on pain of being held negligent before the eternal Judge himself.

In the course of his Latin work on the *Truth of the Holy Scriptures*, Wyclif makes frequent reference to the responsibility of the clergy for the proclamation of God's law. All Christians, he says, and especially clergy, together with the bishops, are held to know, before everything else, the whole law of Scripture. This follows, he maintains, from the law of charity, according to which we ought to love God above all and our neighbors as ourselves. Such love for God and ourselves, however, is impossible aside from adherence to the divine legislation.

The very peace of nations is impossible without the promulgation of this law, which it is the priest's high office to declare. Christ's admonition to all men to seek first the Kingdom of God and his justice provides the prime requisite without which the true life of the Church cannot be nurtured. Any traditional course of ecclesiastical action, which tends to impede the free scope of this evangelical pronouncement, is, therefore, an impingement on the Church's very existence.

Preaching the Word of God is the proper response of the priest to Christ, who called upon Peter to feed His sheep. All the faithful have a priestly duty in winning souls for salvation; in so doing they too are begetting spiritual sons of the Church. But such engendering of spiritual progeny is the special duty and opportunity of those called by Christ to the office of preaching. Thus it is that out of the laws of charity and faith there arises the sacerdotal responsibility that embraces the work of preaching. Upon this the priestly dignity depends. Wyclif says, unhesitatingly, that the preaching of God's Word is a work of greater religious significance than the celebration of the Eucharist. II Timothy emphasizes the necessity of preaching as indispensable to the priestly office; in fact, one cannot be a true priest without the proper knowledge and distribution of Scriptural truth. It behooves every spiritual pastor to have knowledge of the Holy Scriptures. A pastor in name is really not a shepherd in fact unless he feeds the sheep. Preaching the Word constitutes just such nourishment of the faithful. No other duty can be given preferred rating in the pastor's life to that demanded of him as the preacher of God's law and of his Kingdom.

After a frank section on the relative insignificance of human legislation and modern laws, Wyclif once more expounds the unique claims of the gospel. To ignore the Scriptures is to ignore Christ, since Christ himself is that Scripture which we ought to know and that faith which we ought to believe. In fact, failure in Scriptural knowledge means exclusion from the Kingdom of God. No sterner injunction to give the Bible its proper place in clerical life can well be imagined. Certainly, if one is to be a priest of Christ, he must study the Master's law and make it available to his people. Only then does he become a true rector and curate.

One of Wyclif's strongest statements involves his declaration that the proper knowledge and teaching of the Scriptures renders virtually unnecessary liturgical books such as the missal, antiphonary, and psalter. It was often implied in Wyclif's day that knowledge of the credo and the paternoster constituted the minimum essentials for pastoral teaching and the knowledge of the faithful. Wyclif, however, took direct issue with all contentions that no further duty of preaching was necessary, once the Symbol and Dominical prayer had been enjoined.

Among other striking emphases of Wyclif's Scriptural program are these: The preoccupation with the form and theme of the sermon is not, itself, the essence of preaching — rather is it the desire to edify the Church with the Word of God. Good living, interpreted according to the most rigid standards of Christian truth, is a sermon in itself. The vernacular sermon alone is truly edifying.

It is interesting to observe that Wyclif capitalizes the argument of I Corinthians as to the difference between speaking in tongues and genuinely edifying the people. Authentic prophesying, such as the latter evinces, is the real requirement placed upon those who would serve the Church. In another section, Wyclif boldly says that the pope has only such rights — whatever may be the pretentions of his papal bulls — as the Scriptures themselves give him. Consequently, one may follow the approbation or reprobation of the pontiff only in so far as these are founded in Scripture.

In Part I, Chapter 13, of Wyclif's book entitled *The Evangelical Work,* he discusses the portion of the Beatitudes that extols mercy. He concludes that preaching is the most excellent form of it. Of all the kinds of knowledge that make possible a release from misery, preaching is chiefest. Current in his day, of course, was the study of letters, medicine, alchemy, astronomy, and philosophy. He held theology, however, to be higher than any of these and subsumed under it that division known as predication, or preaching. It was best and most noble of all. In the ensuing chapter he gives a long summation from Grosseteste. The passage arrives at the conclusion already observed by Wyclif, namely, that true presentation of the gospel shall be assessed as a reward to its announcer on the Day of Judgment. It is Grosseteste's belief, also, that theology does outrank all other sciences. And he presents the claims of this subject as one that so looks to the future as to help to transform the present.

Chrysostom is frequently quoted as to the duty of prelates, for instance, in Part I, Chapter 21, of *The Evangelical Work.* In this and succeeding portions, Wyclif demonstrates how necessary is a good life in the pulpit, and out of it, if Christ's disciples are to give the proper saltiness to the faithful that their function requires.

Wyclif puts the case thus in a sermon on " Christ Preaching at Nazareth ": " Surely travail of the preacher, or the name of having of good understanding should not be the end of preaching, but profit to the souls of the people. And however this end cometh best, is most pleasing to God. And curious preaching of Latin is full far from this end, for many preach themselves, and fail to preach Jesus Christ; and so sermons do less good than they did in meek times " (50:255).

The " Senses " of Scripture Interpretation

But what of the different senses in which Scripture might be interpreted? Origen had, of course, permitted of a bodily or historical — that is, a literal — sense, even as he thought of a moral sense, to be equated with that of the soul. He considered, also, a higher, spiritual meaning. This was allegorical or mystical.

The medieval world thought increasingly of literal, allegorical, moral, and anagogical senses. A typical handbook of the Middle Ages speaks in terms of the historical or literal, the tropological or moral, the allegorical, and the anagogical or mystical.

Robert Grant, in *The Bible in the Church,* reproduces from the invaluable studies of Caplan and others the heart of the ruling classifications. He sets forth a later mnemonic device by which the older medieval categories were recalled:

" The letter shows us what God and our fathers did;
The allegory shows us where our faith is hid.
The moral meaning gives us rules of daily life;
The anagogy shows us where we end our strife."

Such a fourfold group of senses proceeded especially from Augustine and Cassian. Jerusalem, for example (Gal. 4:22 ff.), has a quadruple meaning: " Historically, it means the city of the Jews; allegorically it signifies the Church of Christ; anagogically it points to that heavenly city which is the mother of us all; and tropologically [or morally] it indicates the human soul."

Wyclif trumpets without wearying against the manner in which " antichrist's tyrants " — the papal hierarchy — and private religionists — i.e., the mendicants — speak against Christ's new law. They " say that literal knowledge of it should never be taken, but spiritual knowledge. And they feign this spiritual knowledge after the wicked will that they have. And thus these four sects are about to destroy literal knowledge of God's law, which should be the first and the most, by which the church should be ruled " (52:259).

Wyclif, to be sure, has his own canon of a truly spiritual meaning. Moses, having received the old law printed on tables of stone, descended from Mount Sinai with shining face. Christ's disciples, having sustained Christ's new law stamped upon their hearts, radiated a glory greater still. " For printing in their souls was better than printing in the stones; and the shining of grace of Christ passed bodily shining in Moses' face " (52:260). But Wyclif is hardly gracious in his appraisal of others' Scriptural interpretation; and his own has a diamond hardness amounting at times to a colorless, if sharp-cutting, edge.

Wyclif follows Augustine in making a place for a sermon to

be read — assuming, of course, that it be in the vernacular. Preaching on Christ's reading and speaking in Luke 4:16 the Englishman says: "Of this deed of Christ men take that it is lawful for to write and afterward to read a sermon, for thus did Christ our Lord and Master; for if men may thus turn the people, what should hinder them to have this manner? " (50:255).

God's Law Variously Proclaimed

In all fairness, not only Wyclif, but many other medieval preachers also, had love of God's law as it united Word and worship.

Thus Augustine, in his sermon on the Symbol, calls for the reduction to memory of that inner law. This unwritten covenant, one even transcending Jer. 31:33, recapitulates the Lord's Scriptural will and the way of true worship.

Maurus' Sabbath law spoke to worshiping hearts the Biblical precepts of the God who created all things in six days and rested on the seventh.

Wulfstan dared to judge the law of men by the law of God, and prognosticated the ruin that must follow any but the divine plan.

Raoul Ardent coupled the Old Testament law of judgment and the New Testament law of love as the emancipating light of the world.

Grosseteste linked Old Testament constitutions, which he sent to his diocesan clerics, and the New Testament evangel, with which he hailed the papal curia into the highest court of the universe.

De Vitry, preaching to laborers on the ancient laws of the Pentateuch, joined work and worship, gospel and liturgy, ecclesiastical accountability and lay obligation.

The mendicants, by no means so devoid of the gospel as Wyclif insinuated, proclaimed the law of evangelical poverty

with the Franciscans and the gospel legislation of truth among
the Dominicans.

The Lollards, often friends of the Church, if not too often
men of the cloth, sounded anew, with vernacular power, the
voice of the " seventy," as they preached the good news of the
" twelve."

Bernardine, master of the canon law, called to the Scriptures
and worship as the united preoccupation that should rule the
soul of every hearer, humble and exalted.

Savonarola brought the law of the prophets and of Yahweh's
impending day as an all-cleansing fire unto the penitent, even
as he awaited, in the humble Christ's return, the regnant Judge
of the cosmos.

Michel Menot showed how to bring into unitive advance the
laws of men and the commands of God; of Old Testament and
New Covenant; of urban masses and rural dispersion; of scholastic orator and popular discourser. Thus they might, with
Isaiah the prophet and Paul the apostle, draw the preacher
and his congregation into the presence of the Holy One and
send them forth together into the service of the oppressed.

The Word and Christ's Mystical Body

Of Scriptural preaching that linked the eternal Word with
the mystical body of Christ there was a medieval abundance.
Francis, in a sermonic exhortation, addressed all Christian
brethren " and all who dwell in the whole world ":

" Being the servant of all, I am bound to serve all and to
administer the balm-bearing words of my Lord."

Then, with his customary dovetailing of Scriptural passages,
he associated, according to orthodox interpretation, the life of
Him who was made flesh among men, the Christian communi-
cating in his sacramental body and blood, and the indispensable
functions of the Church's priesthood. " This Word of the Father

. . . when His Passion was nigh, . . . celebrated the Pasch with His disciples and, taking bread, He gave thanks and blessed and broke saying: *Take ye and eat: this is My Body.* And, taking the chalice, He said: *This is My Blood of the New Testament, which shall be shed for you and for many unto remission of sins* (Matt. 26:26–28). . . . Such was the will of the Father that His Son, Blessed and Glorious, whom He gave to us, and who was born for us, should by His own Blood, sacrifice, and oblation, offer Himself on the altar of the Cross, not for Himself, by whom *all things were made* (John 1:3), but for our sins, leaving us an example that we should follow His steps " (35:182).

Francis says, further: " We ought indeed to confess all our sins to a priest and receive from him the Body and Blood of our Lord Jesus Christ. He who does not eat His Flesh and does not drink His Blood cannot enter into the Kingdom of God. . . . And let us all know for certain that no one can be saved except by the Blood of our Lord Jesus Christ and by the holy words of the Lord which clerics say and announce and distribute and they alone administer and not others." The utmost Catholicity, as connoted by the Church in his day, is here called for, not only inferentially, but also specifically. As in so many other connections, he says, " We ought . . . to be Catholics " (35:183–184).

John Tauler, who died just after the middle of the fourteenth century, preached a remarkable sermon on spiritual deafness to the eternal Word. It begins:

" We are to inquire to-day into man's spiritual deafness. Since our first parents lent a willing ear to the voice of Satan, we are all deaf to the voice of the eternal Word of God within our souls. And yet we know full well that this divine Word is indescribably close to our souls, closer than our own thoughts, or our very nature to our conscious existence. Within our inmost souls dwells that divine Word, and He addresses us without ceasing. Man hears Him not, for he is afflicted with great deafness. Nor is this a blameless state of deafness, for we are like one to whom something is spoken, and who stops his ears lest he shall hear what it is. We are worse; we have done this so much that at last we have lost knowledge of ourselves, and are become dumb, that is to say, wholly stupid " (48: 246–247).

Tauler's analysis of how this deafness comes about through man's tragic fostering of the ear that hears not, and his suggestions as to the means of detecting the malady and then rendering the self open to the Lord's healing touch, constitute a masterpiece of religious literature. The Lord's act of blessed restoration so that the soul can once more hear and speak is a moving tribute to the divine redemptiveness through the love of God's Son.

Nicholas of Cusa of the fifteenth century, preaching a sermon on the Eucharist, states succinctly the medieval conviction concerning the union of the preached Word and the ministry of worship.

" Thence it comes that Christ offers himself as the bread of life to those discerning spirits of ours, which, through victory over sensible things, deliver themselves captive through faith, and without doubt believe that to be true which sense denies. Such a result, indeed, proceeds from this alone, that [the spirit] believes him, whom it sees a man, to be the Son of God. In consequence of this faith, it believes all that the Son pronounces and preaches as the words of God, to whom nothing is impossible. . . . This faith shows, moreover, that the bread of the Gospel has the knowledge of life, since it is the word of eternal life and shows also, since it is the only food of life, the justification of the incarnate word [in its two aspects], of preaching and of the justifying host. . . . Therefore, as he himself was sent by the Father, minister of the word of life which he possessed, ministering the sustenance of life, and offering himself as that sustenance; just so he sent the apostles and disciples and their successors to the end of the ages in the same way as he himself was sent by the Father, that they also, in the word of life, might minister the food of life . . . in the form of corporeal foods. And thus you see how the sustenance of life should be administered in preaching just as in oblation. And the preaching is so much the more perfect, in proportion to the fruitfulness and the frequency in it of that sweetest oblation, the mystical body of Christ" (57:289–290).

Well might Cusa, the scholar and teacher of primary sources, say in another sermon: " The Word made flesh summons this intellectual life through grace to fellowship with the Word, through which it tastes, in the fountain of the Father, the sweetness of his divine life, which is imparted to the sons of God" (58:294).

THE WORD, LITURGY, AND COMMUNION OF SAINTS

There remains, now, the necessity of indicating, finally, how the divine Word in the liturgy brought to life the Church's calendar in the larger communion of saints; how the Church, militant, suffering, and triumphant, was indisseverably joined, through Word and worship.

A sermon " On All Saints " that stubbornly resists all divorcement from the Venerable Bede is a joyously sober paean of triumph (17:108–109):

" To-day, beloved, we celebrate in the joy of one solemnity, the Festival of All Saints: in whose companionship the heaven exults; in whose guardianship the earth rejoices; by whose triumphs Holy Church is crowned; whose confession, as braver in its passion, is also brighter in its honour — because, while the battle increased, the glory of them that fought in it was also augmented. And the triumph of martyrdom is adorned with the manifold kind of its torments, because the more severe the pangs, the more illustrious also were the rewards; while our Mother, the Catholic Church, was taught by her Head, Jesus Christ, not to fear contumely, affliction, death; and more and more strengthened, — not by resistance, but by endurance, — inspired all of that illustrious number who suffered imprisonment or torture, with one and equal ardour to fight the battle, for triumphal glory. . . .

"With how joyous a breast the heavenly city receives those that return from fight! How happily she meets them that bear the trophies of the conquered enemy! With triumphant men, women also come, who rose superior both to this world and to their sex, doubling the glory of their warfare; virgins with youths, who surpassed their tender years by their virtues. Yet not they alone, but the rest of the multitude of the faithful shall also enter the palace of that eternal court, who in peaceful union have observed the heavenly commandments, and have maintained the purity of the faith.

"Now, therefore, brethren, let us enter the way of life; let us return to the celestial city, in which we are citizens, enrolled and inscribed. For we are *no more strangers and foreigners, but fellow-citizens of the saints, and of the household of God — heirs of God, and joint-heirs with Christ* (Eph. 2:19; Rom. 8:17)."

Bernard of Clairvaux, speaking of that heritage that will be re-established only when the "heirs of it return to their first state," celebrates the blessedness of the martyrs: "Each of them indeed received a white robe; but they will not be vested in a second, until we too shall be vested with them. We hold as pledges and hostages their very bodies, without which their glory cannot be consummated, nor will they receive those until the time when we shall receive ours with them " (27:147–148).

Invoking the imagery of Heb. 11:40, the great Cistercian preacher cries out:

" O if we could comprehend with what earnest and eager desire they expect and await our coming! . . . Hasten, then, my brethren, hasten; for not the Angels alone, but the Creator of the Angels awaits you. The marriage feast is prepared, but the house is not yet full of guests: those who shall fill the places at the feast are still being waited for. The Father awaits you. . . . Will . . . [the Son] not bring back to communion with Him, His creatures, for whose sake the Father sent Him into the world? The Holy Spirit also awaits us. . . . Since then the wedding feast is prepared, and all the hosts of the heavenly court are waiting for and desiring our coming: let us, my brethren, run our Christian course not as uncertainty, let us run with earnest desire, and striving after virtue " (27:148–149).

Unto that Kingdom of Heaven, Thomas Aquinas prays that the faithful may come. Anticipating the joys of the Heavenly City, he longs for the fairness and goodness of the angelic society, " for angels [too] are its citizens. . . . They who are in that city celebrate a perpetual feast. . . . S. Augustine, in his book on the City of God, says, *If it is asked, What is the occupation of this city? we say, that there we shall take rest, and shall see, and shall love, and shall praise, and shall sing. For what else shall be our end unless we come to that kingdom, of which there will be no end* " (43:227–228).

THE NEED FOR JOINING WORD AND WORSHIP TODAY

Perhaps with some of these views we shall, today, be unable to associate our spiritual inclinations. But for their intimate conjunction of Scriptural Word and divine worship we shall hardly enter a complete demurrer. Perchance, to some fair degree, at least, we may say:

The clear testimony of the Christian ministry recognizes the priority of worship if God is to be served, Christ enthroned, and men saved. Worship comes first and last. Jesus exemplified, and Paul preached, as he practiced, that Word and worship are immutably joined.

The power of the golden-tongued Chrysostom lay in his summoning the people, under the spell of the gospel word, to the supreme act of divine worship. Calvin preached and taught so that the Christian flock might assimilate the gospel message and be ready to receive the Spirit that indwelt in communal worship. Francis of Assisi in the thirteenth century, Luther in the sixteenth, and Rufus Jones in the twentieth, manifested — though in widely different ways — one common Christian conviction. This was that the supreme duty of the minister is not to practice or to inculcate feverish, human busyness. It is, first, to be still and know that God reigns forevermore. Each in his own way proved also — as did Rauschenbusch and hundreds more — that they who worship in unself-conscious reverence are, of all men, the most irrevocably committed to human service when the hour of action strikes.

Well did Martin Luther come to realize that, not in proud achievements of his own doing, but in private prayer and corporate worship, would true reformation come — and the salvation of mankind with it. What mountains of human impossibility he moved in the faith and power gained there, the whole world knows. How contritely did the mature Wesley repent the stiff-necked activism of his earlier days as he bowed his knees to the Father in his later communing with God and his people! And how strikingly were the fruits of his active life traceable to the tree of worship!

Today, uncalculating worship of the divine, entered into for nought but the confession of sin and the praise of the Lord's graciousness is, as always, the Christian's most inescapable and joyously opportune responsibility. This is the one adequate basis of world communion. This is what Amsterdam served to clarify, if it shed any light that is to be truly enduring. For this end the periodic re-examination of the Church's true nature in Christ is intended. To this goal of unimpeded fellowship with the only one rightly called Master, laity and clergy together move. This message, and not some novel plaything of power politicians, is the hope for one world. This, and not some union of burnished technology with polished, humanistic unction, is the inheritor of the new heaven and the new earth.

What the Christian preacher and teacher may humbly, yet radiantly, proclaim in propagating it is clearly revealed in the benediction of Jesus' consecration prayer; it is resplendent with the glory of his sure victory over the world. And never so transformingly as in the eucharistic Communion — reminiscent of that agape long ago — does the love Christ then showed forth envelop the whole world still.

Here, indeed, those called unto everlasting brotherhood have union such as that of Father, Son, and Holy Spirit. Called to an interpenetrating communion not that of the world, they continue to dwell in the world as a heaven-yeasted, earth-transforming leaven. Here the preachers of the gospel receive the eternal Word for communication to the faithful; here the Lord's true people give back their echo of his own mighty voice. Joined together in a diversity of ministries, lent to one vast unity of saving faith, hope, and love, they cease not to cry aloud the Lord's redemptiveness. Their trumpets of praise and adoration send forth, victoriously, " no uncertain sound."